The Resurrected Frog

By

Sylvia J. Cohen

ISBN: 1-4033-2383-6 (E-book)
ISBN: 1-4033-2384-4 (Paperback)

This book is printed on acid free paper.

1stBooks - rev. 07/01/02

Acknowledgments

Special thanks to Beverly and Victor Deutsch and Family. The doors of your home are full of welcome. How precious thou art.

Special thanks to Kathy Muraviov. You stepped in on time and picked up the broken pieces. Your kindness will never be underrated. Many will see you for your services.

Dedication

Special thanks to Bishop NL Wagner and Dr. Ernest Perry. Your reward is in Heaven. To my clergymen and Saints of the Most High God— "The prayer of a righteous availeth much." To my immediate family—if we pray together, we will stay together.

Foreword

Frog: Smooth-skinned, web-footed, largely aquatic, tailless, agile, leaping amphibian.

Frog-Kick: A breast stroke kick executed with the knees turned outward and the legs separated and then swung together. Frog legs are considered an edible delicacy.

Why *The Resurrected Frog*? It derived from my being too embarrassed to tell anyone about my past. Many events lay deep down in my heart and it would take the Lord Jesus to encourage me to write and tell this true story. He assured me He would purge the things I couldn't face or even answer, such as why all this happened to me. It took years to write this and at times, as my mind regressed, the agony and pain would overwhelm me. God purged and cleansed my lost soul. Now I realize my life is in His hands. Suffering endures for a night, and as I can attest, joy will come in the morning. As you read my story, there may be times you'll laugh or cry, but I implore you, do not see me as that nasty frog, but rather see me as one who is sought after for the delicacy.

Introduction

I was recently listening to a woman who had encountered many abuses, both as a child and later in her adult life, during her marriage. As she spoke, she hammered away at so many things concerning "child abuse," that, I, too, was ministered to by her ability to expose such embarrassing events. I felt overwhelmed in my heart as she chipped away at the hidden agony, deep within me of my own past experiences. And how dare she stand there recovered while she was uncovering me and my private secrets.

As she spoke, she told a story about being a young girl. "I remember as a child going on a field trip and we were permitted to bring our favorite pet or animal for a show-and-tell contest. I didn't have a pet or animal. I found a frog hopping on one leg, so I placed him in a jar, just to have something for the contest."

Surely, I thought, a lame frog with one leg couldn't win any prize.

She continued on. "As soon as we got to the campgrounds, I ran and placed my frog on the picnic table in the hot sun with some of the other entrants. That evening after hiking, we gathered for the contest. I was the first to show my pet as I held the jar in my hands, but the frog appeared listless—in fact, it was dead. So a few girls and I conducted a real funeral for him. We dug a hole in the ground and wrapped him in a cloth, then laid him in his shallow grave. Just about the time we were to finish our show-and-tell, someone yelled, 'Look!' The ground shook and out jumped the frog we had buried, on one foot."

As she was finishing this part of the story, I yelled, leaping from my seat, "A resurrected frog!" With tears flowing down my cheeks, the speaker walked over, and hugging me, gave me the poem which begins my story.

The story of the frog seemingly coming back from the dead renewed for me the resurrection story, and revealed the wonderful insight that though many things may seem dead in our lives—and indeed they are both dead and buried—there is a power which can catapult us above and beyond our past grave of life's circumstances to a new awakening and opportunity—a second chance, a new beginning, *a resurrection*.

This pain is the flame of a fire,
    burning out of control.
It has eaten away at my heart
    right down to my very soul
I'll build a wall around me,
    so the fire can't get in.
My heart's been burnt to ashes,
    so much ugliness within.
Lord, give me beauty for ashes
    Teach me to live again.
Only you can squelch the fire,
    burning me from within.
Lord, give me beauty for ashes,
    replace the old with new.
Renew my heart and show me how,
    my healing can serve you.

Prologue

I wonder as I look back over my life, how I made it to this age, fifty-eight, looking toward seeing fifty-nine. I don't mind telling my age, for God has blessed and kept me. Even the scars I received from birth until now are hardly visible. If you were to meet me, you wouldn't be able to tell or guess what storms or trials I have endured throughout my life. Only as you read, will you know and ask, "How could Sylvia go that long before she realized she needed help?"

One of the reasons for sharing this story is, I want young people to understand they do not have to make a mess out of their lives. Dad and Mom are there for you—or perhaps are not—and yes, we can get caught up on the wrong road, but be well-assured that whether we have support from parents or not, I declare unto you that Jesus is the way and He can help you. It is imperative you acknowledge Him and turn from where you are—do it now! He will help you find the road which will make a better life.

Chapter 1

At fifteen years old, the month of September was the first time I would enter Hillman Junior High School. Full of excitement, I knew new adventures awaited me, especially without the security Mom and Dad had provided me up until now. Skipping along the street headed toward the school, I caught up with some of the neighbor kids, Bar, Vern, and Etta. We moved swiftly, yet not in a rush, all excited and enthusiastic about our first day in junior high. As we walked, we chattered on about our class schedules and the different homerooms we each had. Finally arriving at school dressed as crisply as cucumbers, equipped with new tablets, and pencils gripped in our hands, we stood waiting for the first bell to ring.

The halls were wider and much longer than the grade school I attended last year. My homeroom was three flights up, Room 303, and there were many more boys and girls from the Upper and Lower Southside. I met and became acquainted with new faces as I made my way to each classroom. My attitude in meeting up with so many boys and girls soon changed since we Southsiders thought we were the best kids in town and held a sort of rivalry and contempt for others who did not reside on our side of town.

September also began the football season for all junior and senior high schools. I could just imagine how much fun there would be attending the games. I often played neighborhood football with my brother and his friends. I remember, not fondly, once being tackled and my face landing in cow manure! My oldest brother Billyboy, accompanied me to most of the games and the different activities throughout the community. Skating and dancing were our Fall and Winter activities.

As with all young people, I had the expectancy of being just beyond the reach of the tight security Mom and Dad had given my adolescent years, until now. During the Spring and Summer we went swimming, hiking, and played baseball games in the great Mill Creek Park. My older sister, Marva, stayed close to home, while I usually ran around with Billyboy.

Marva was the oldest of six children, Billyboy was second, and I, the black sheep of the family, was third, with a younger sister,

Connie, and two brothers, Eric and Vernon, after her. Each one of us had our own personalities. But being in the middle I was somehow different than my sister and brothers. My views and the way I saw things just didn't add up like the rest of the family. Marva was more of a young lady, and I was more of a tomboy. I loved to run with my brother, climbing trees, hiking in the woods, and playing baseball or football games. I was not like Marva, who stayed close to home, studying or tending to chores, and unfortunately, it wasn't until her death in 1974 that I realized how much I loved my sister, who died in her early thirties of cancer.

Leechburg, Pennsylvania, was the place of my birth, about sixty-eight miles east of Youngstown, Ohio. I was the only child born in a home my father built with his bare hands. He dug through slate with his pick and shovel forming the foundation and laid the bricks which constructed the frame of the new home. I loved that place called Eilson Hill. It was a wooded area which overlooked the town of Leechburg. There was so much more clean fun and fresh air compared to Youngstown. Y-town, as Youngstown can be called, had steel mills which ran east and west of the Mahoning River. There was always the smell of Dad's job in the air, which had brought our family to Youngstown. It seems to me, my life would have ended up differently had we remained in Leechburg.

My birth had been a difficult one. I was born on July 4th with my umbilical cord wrapped around my little neck causing me to be born what's called a blue baby. The doctor, who was actually a horse doctor, pronounced me dead at birth. I'm told he'd cut the cord from around my neck and tried to revive me, but failed. He then pushed me into a corner with no hope of my surviving. My dad said that sometime early the next morning, July 5th, I began to cry and I've been crying ever since. A miracle child some would say, others, just happenstance. But God was in it somewhere.

My difficult birth was to be a sign for my whole life which would be a road full of troubles. It seemed everything that should have been good for me, turned out ugly. Mom said even as a baby, I would cry seemingly for no reason. As time passed, she found out I was actually a sickly child, born with Sickle Cell Anemia, which caused me to suffer from earaches, joint pain, dehydration, and all that went along with having this disease. August was always a bad month for me because the pain in my body would become so excruciating. Seemingly each year that followed, the pain would worsen—and during my teenage years, the pain was unbearable.

My first night at the football game was so exciting. At the gate I remembered walking through and paying the attendant 50 cents. I could see and hear many people who had already come from all over the city to watch the South High football team. We moved quickly to the bleachers and sat midway on the northwest side, the side of which most of our team sat and cheered.

I noticed a man whom I had seen just a few days ago as I stood on my porch waiting for my classmates to walk to school. We were not taught to ignore folks, but instead to be kind. So I would give him a smile each morning when he would make a stop at the corner of Cleveland Street and Edwards, at the stop sign. As he was sitting here at the game, having seen his face before, I acknowledged him and then continued with the crowd to cheer our team. Throughout the game, our group laughed and made remarks together, just plain having fun. The man and I sat four benches apart, and he would turn to look up at us and make congenial remarks. When the game was over we all went our separate ways. The next time I would see this man was the following Wednesday after choir rehearsal.

Going to church before we could participate in any other activities was one of our parental requirements. Singing was always an activity I enjoyed. We'd finished rehearsing when the choir directress called to me and asked if I could stay for a few minutes to work with her on a new song. Then I heard someone say, "Your *friend* is outside waiting for you." I remember telling one of my brothers, "Bill, wait for me—I want to walk home with you and the others." I didn't want to miss the great fun we all had on our way home together.

When I stepped outside they were already on their way so I felt the need to run to catch up with them. A car horn blew and as I turned, I remembered what had been said to me, *"A friend was outside waiting."* As I looked, I noticed it was the man from the ball game, the same one I often greeted as he stopped at the stop sign. I walked over to the car to see what he wanted.

"Get in—I'll take you to meet up with your friends. Come on, I won't bite you," he said as he reached over and opened the car door.

Cooking, making beds, washing clothes, sweeping the floor, and sometimes babysitting were my duties as a young girl. Mom and Dad taught us to work hard in school so we wouldn't have to bring our school work home. They often told us to be good at whatever we did. I can still hear my mom.

"Sylvia, whatever you turn out to be, be good at that. If you are a bum, be the best bum you can be." She'd also tell me, "Keep your dress down." Now why would she say a thing like that? I didn't go around with my dress up in the air! It never made sense.

For clean fun, we played with the neighbor kids in the street or up in the Catholic field about a block away from home, and at times that was too far from home for us. Sometimes while playing we could hear our parents calling out to one of us when we were wanted at home. There were times our parents needed us to come home in order to go somewhere with them; other times, the call seemed more urgent. You could tell if there was trouble by the tone of a parent's voice. We would often make fun if we heard a distress call. We'd sing, *"You're in trouble now, you're gonna get it!"* Then we'd all laugh out loud. On occasion, sometimes we wouldn't see that friend for a few days and then we would worry and wonder if something bad had really happened. I recall a time when one boy's parents had beat him something awful. He had to remain in the house for weeks before anyone saw him. His dad was an alcoholic and that, too, was part of life we learned to accept as children. To see an alcoholic stumble and fall down the street cursing and spitting was one of the nastiest things we saw or knew. Yet as children we were told by Mom and Dad it was none of our business. Having not seen this boy for a while, we all sat on one of the neighbor's porches, praying in our own way. Someone might be heard to say, "Lord, let him be all right." After we saw or heard that he was okay, we would then go back to our normal selves, playing and poking at each other.

I started a singing group with my best friend Bar, my brother Billyboy, my cousin Ronnie, and their friends, Willie and Donald. We called ourselves "The Hightones." Our voices blended really well together. We'd dress in powder blue sweaters with white buckskin shoes and navy skirts for the girls, and navy trousers for the boys. We traveled locally and won first place in most of the contests we entered.

4

"Sylvia, don't make a mess out of this and throw it all away," my brother remarked to me because we were doing so well at one time. He didn't realize we were all changing and anything could happen to anyone—as it soon did.

Billyboy was already in junior high school, as were Ronnie and Willie. Bar and I were just in sixth grade, headed for junior high that following Fall. As part of the Hightones we had to be chaperoned at all times or stay close to the boys of the group. Most of our protection came from the boys we sang with during our performing engagements. We were just plain, ordinary kids with no television to teach us life's trials. Dope was a word that meant slow or dumb, although it still means that today. The dirtiest word we may have used to curse with was so minimal by today's standards, it would not be considered foul language. We lived in a state of true innocence.

Ronnie, who was my cousin, friend, and dance partner—we were so close, many thought I was either his sister or his girlfriend. Every Friday and Saturday evening there were socials all around the neighborhood where the boys and girls gathered in the basement of someone's home to socialize. We paid for entrance to either dance or eat. It was there I met Brandon Matthews—who would later become part of my life—in the living room of a home on Marion Street. I often saw him at Reed's Arena where we would occasionally go to skate.

Rivalry was common among the boys and girls who lived in Youngstown. I met many of my acquaintances at either a social or the skating rink. One person who comes to mind was Jerome, from the North Side. I was too young to call myself in love with any of them, but I did like Jerome. I also was not permitted to date, not at thirteen. At best, I was permitted a few telephone calls, supervised by my parents.

"Sylvia, get the phone. You have five minutes and then hang up." Either my parents or older sister or brother stood around listening.

There was one neighboring family who didn't have a father who lived in the home, as we did. They had their problems, but kept them to themselves. The two sisters had the responsibility to help rear the younger siblings and they did their best to "train up a child in the way he shall go and when he is old, he will not depart from it." (Ps. 22:6) Today those children hold respectful jobs in the community.

5

One of the daughters from that family became pregnant and when she shared her secret with me, I laughed, not knowing laughing can be catching. At this time, a girl pregnant out of wedlock was a disgrace to not only the family, but the whole neighborhood. She carried a child without anyone knowing, right up to the time of delivery. After getting dressed for school, she started down the steps intending to go to class when she was hit with a pain and went into labor. She only had enough time to lay down on the couch at the base of the steps where she gave birth to a baby boy. Her mother found her with the baby laying at her feet. The way it was told, the girl's mother looked at the baby, and seeing the newborn, passed out.

Chapter 2

That young girl's experience should have been an example for all the girls in our neighborhood. We weren't the kind of kids one would call bad, and neither did we practice the things which would bring disgrace on our families. But that big bad wolf, the fellow who cared little about the good training we had, so long as he could catch one of us girls out alone—would patiently wait to bait a trap for us. Yes, I was one of the ones who got caught in a mess. All that people would later label me just was not so. I was called words like "whore," "prostitute," and all the names that go with an unwed pregnancy. But I hadn't even finished playing with dolls and mud pies when this ungodly thing happened to me.

Every Wednesday, after school, my sister and brothers and I went to choir rehearsal. I was asked by the choir director to remain a few minutes to go over a lead part. It was then that someone said a friend was waiting outside in a car for me. I thought, who could this be? In a car waiting for me? I had no friends with a car.

Curious to know what he wanted, I approached the car. *Oh, it's the man from the football game,* I thought. "Yes," I asked, "what do you want with me?" I hesitated as he reached over opening up the car door.

"Get in and I'll drive you up the hill to your friends."

I hesitated. He seemed harmless enough. I got into his car and looked him over. "Hey, what's your name?" I asked as I looked to see if I could find something which would indicate he might not be a good person.

"Ah, my name is Robert and I want to get acquainted with you. You're Sylvia." With that, he turned and looked me right in the face. "I asked and was told all about you," as if reading my thoughts.

"Who told you what?"

"Look, I'll drive you up to meet your friends, okay? I can get there faster than your pretty little legs can carry you. Sit back," he instructed as he reached across my legs to shut the door. "I understand you can sing. How about a song for me? We'll see the kids on High Street, won't we? Sit back and relax."

"Maybe I don't want to go with you." I turned to open the door, but the car pulled away from the corner and moved toward High Street.

"Girl, sit back. I ain't gonna hurt you."

Seeing the kids, I yelled, "There they are! Let me out!" The dogface drove right past my friends!

"Oh, grow up, child. Don't you want to know who I am? I'll just go up the block and park. We'll wait until they pass by, then you can get out. I've watched you walk this route many a time."

By now we'd arrived at school off Edwards Street and parked under a streetlight on Thornton Street. I wasn't certain what was going to happen, nor what was going on in his mind, but I knew I was in trouble with my parents if they ever found out I was sitting in this car with a complete stranger.

"Now what harm can I do you sitting under these lights? Let's just talk and learn about one another. Is that okay with you? Come over a little closer, I can hardly hear your voice." He began to pull and tug.

I sat with my hands across my chest in an attitude of disagreement.

"If you won't come to me, I'll come over there and you won't like that." He moved closer to me and put his arms around my shoulders. I was perplexed and not sure what to do.

"Get your arms off my body and let's just talk," I heard my own timid voice say. I could feel my heart beat against my chest. I was scared. He'd already begun to be forceful. With his face in front of mine, he kissed me. His tongue reached down, it seemed, to the back of my throat. His lips clung to my lips like glue. I could not say a word. Then he maneuvered me under him with his strong arms. With his mouth locked to my lips, he forced me to lay under him. My little head was pinned between the car door and the seat, with his forearm across my neck, cutting off my breath. I struggled and then whatever went on, I don't know because I passed out. When I came to, I only remember him brushing my clothes back in place and asking, "Are you all right?"

"Yes, what time is it?" For that split-second I thought, *I must be in trouble with my parents. What will I tell them?* Looking for an excuse, I remembered I had to stay with the directress to rehearse a song. Mom and Dad very seldom talked to those directors anyhow. The moisture in my undergarments did not indicate to me what had just taken place. After all, my clothes were still in place. I never saw anything unusual, nor had I felt any penetration. My body was numb, just as I remembered it being before. I only wanted to go home, to security. Little did I know what had just taken place with this man, Robert. But I soon would.

When lust has conceived, it brings forth sin. I had not lusted, but still was in sin. I knew something had happened because within that first week, I felt my body change. My mother, too, sensed something because I was sleeping so much. And so she carted me off to the doctor.

"Sylvia, you're pregnant," were the doctor's stinging words.

My mind could not fathom what he meant. Pregnant, expecting a baby! How? From where? I was fifteen.

*Therefore being justified by faith, we have peace with God through our Lord Jesus Christ: By whom also we have access by faith into this grace wherein which we stand and rejoice in hope of glory of God. And not only so, but we glory in tribulations also: knowing that tribulation worketh patience; And patience, experience; and experience, hope: And hope maketh not ashamed, because the love of God is shed abroad in our hearts by the Holy Ghost who is given unto us. (*Rom. 5:1-5)

Chapter 3

During the hearing in court, Robert lied. He'd also gotten to Brandon—the one I'd met in the living room of the social—and paid him to say he and others had sex with me. Had he not done this, Robert would have been charged with statutory rape since he was eight years older than I.

I suffered the agony and embarrassment of carrying an unwanted child. My name was mud in the neighborhood. Mom and Dad could hardly look upon me as their child. I guess they were also embarrassed and suffered the pain of having their daughter talked about so furiously, but there were people who at one time or another, gave their opinion about me. I can still hear them say, "I told you so!" And yet, there were those, such as my best friend, who tried to encourage me. Bar confessed to me in later years.

"Syl, the only way I got by was because I couldn't get pregnant." She never did have a child.

Just to look at me angered my father and he would verbally and physically attack me. I was constantly accused of things I didn't do or say. One evening I'd cooked supper and my brother was to do his share of the cleaning. He complained about it not being his turn, so vehemently and insistently that I received the brunt of it. I caught my father's fist on my face. Dad's anger got out of control as he continued to swing, and landed many blows to my body. To dodge the beating, I reached for his legs and held tight, making it hard for him to get a good grip on me.

"Dad, please stop! You're hurting me!"

This went on day after day, month after month. I remember, one time, to save myself after Dad started attacking me, I literally dove out a kitchen window. Dad stormed out the back door into the yard searching for me, but I was literally frozen to the earth—between his car's back wheel and the curb. He ran back and forth past me, searching everywhere, but never did see me. Thank God! I stayed frozen in place until he finally ran into the house. I knew he was getting his car keys. I got up and took off running, as fast as my legs would carry me, toward downtown. My legs would not stop. I ran

down Edwards Street, over to High Street and over to Oakhill Avenue. Running, crazy, hating what was happening to me.

I was pregnant!

Thoughts came to my mind as I approached Reed's Skating Arena on the corner of Marshall and Oakhill. *Head to the bridge and jump over.* I entertained the thought. *Go girl, hurry and jump.* And as my bad luck continued, there in front of me, was Robert. He was helping his girlfriend into the car which was parked in the path which led to the bridge, only a few feet away. Seeing me running, he stepped out from his car and caught me. I felt his arm around my belly as he squeezed, holding me tight, my legs kicking the air.

"Let me go!" I yelled with tears streaming down my face.

"Go where? Don't make me slap you, Sylvia," he spoke with concern.

I pushed away from him with anger. "Get your hands off my baby! Get away from me! Leave me alone!"

He insisted, "Not until you promise me you won't run. Anyhow, what are you trying to do, kill yourself? That's my baby and you're going to take care of it. Now stop!" He lifted his hand up over my head as if to hit me. By now I had come to my senses.

"Why don't you ride with me and let's talk?" he asked. Then he turned to his girlfriend. "Why don't you get another ride."

The girl, of course, had heard everything Robert had said and shoot me a questioning look, as if to say, *"Is it his?"*

It seemed he was planted in that spot just to save me, but if I could have, I would have foolishly done something to him that night. Don't ask me why, but I took him up on his offer and got into his car. On the ride home, I told him what Dad had done to me that night.

"Look," he said, "if things get real bad, let me know and I'll see what I can do. You know your parents aren't too fond of me anyhow. Go into the house. I'll ride around to make sure they won't bring you more trouble tonight."

The next day I was sent to my Aunt Jesse's home. She was one of my mother's sisters who lived on the east side of town. I was now about four months pregnant. Aunt Jesse had also gone through the same experience of having a child out of wedlock and had gone to a sanitation home because she had Tuberculosis. It was here that I learned a lot of what it meant to be clean and to clean up. I enjoyed

11

being with my cousin Bertha, my aunt's only child. We became close and at times she was the only one with whom I could talk. I shared many thoughts with her. Up to this point, I'd sit at home with no one to talk to, yet it did give me a chance to speak with the Spirit of God.

It was during my fifth month of pregnancy when one morning upon awakening I was very sick. I continuously vomited. My aunt called my family and they told her to meet them at Southside Hospital. My appendix had been inflamed and needed to come out. Maybe this would be a way of escape and things could go back to normal. But, it never got to that point. While at the hospital, a surgeon examined me and ordered surgery, stat. During the preparation, the doctor asked me if I wanted to keep the baby that had now taken on life in my belly. Just thinking that another being was depending on me to bring it forth to live in this cruel world, I held my stomach and said, "Yes, I want this baby, it's mine." The doctor couldn't guarantee me and said he would spare me over the baby, but assured me he'd do his best to save us both.

After the operation I was placed in a private room. A few days later, while eating lunch, Aunt Jesse and Uncle Mack, Aunt Jesse's husband, came to visit. As we talked, I started slurring my words. My tongue began to get heavy and seemed to push its way out of my mouth. My aunt quickly went out to the nurse's desk for help.

"What's wrong, Sylvia?" the nurse asked as she entered the room.

By now I could hardly utter a word—and soon after that, I was undergoing many tests. By that evening after being examined by at least five doctors none of which could explain what was happening. To keep me from biting my tongue, wires and clamps were placed over my teeth to hold my bite grip back. Only the immediate family was allowed into my room. The lights were lowered as if it were my last day on Earth. That night I opened my eyes and saw the most amazing sight. My room was aglow in a yellowish-amber light that shrunk to the size of a golf ball. As I watched, I pulled the covers off. I jumped, landing my feet on the cold floor, reaching out as to catch it, but the ball moved towards the window. To my surprise, it went out and up to the sky. The doctor walked into my room and caught me standing at the window looking up towards the sky.

"I see you are doing better from last night. I'll check your chart. You can go home later today." The doctor was, needless to say, amazed by my recovery. It was days later when I finally completely recovered. Whatever it was, the sickness that had taken over my body only a few days earlier, seemed to mysteriously disappear.

Mom and Dad took me back home. Things were far better than before, but I still had four more months to go before I was due to deliver the baby growing inside me. I sat quietly and waited, lonely again as all get out. For some reason, I wasn't angry with anyone about how I was treated. There were times I'd see friends in passing or go to a movie—but going to the movies was short-lived. A man in the theater who was sitting behind me had committed a lewd act—I got up and left, never to return again.

"Sylvia," my mother would say, "aren't you tired of sitting around this house? Go to a movie."

This suggestion was supposed to make me less lonely, but I could not find my happiness in a theater where *those* people surely were.

My friend Brandon Matthews phoned several times and said he was in the Army. He said that he was against the thought of me marrying the baby's father, which, believe me, was far from ever happening. He also said not to marry anyone until he talked to me. That meant nothing to me, but it did get me thinking. Marriage would make things better. And I did think of how soft and gentle Brandon was as we danced at the social gatherings—but we were kids, so marriage definitely was not in the cards.

Willie, my brother's friend, had a sister who gave me a baby shower and I received a few gifts. There were times my Uncle Larry would come over and voice his opinion and advice.

"You're not a little girl anymore. When you have this baby, you'll be considered a woman."

I wish I could have said things to my uncle like, "Well, I guess I went from a girl to a woman the night I was molested at the Villiams's home." Let's see then, I must have been a woman at the age of eight, many years before I was raped.

SECURITY: Freedom from danger. Another word is PROTECTION: Measures taken to guard against espionage or sabotage, crime, attack, or escape.

13

Chapter 4

Looking back, reminiscing about when I was eight years old, it seems to me I was molested, and for that same reason, became a woman—having had my first sexual experience with a neighbor man.

I often visited the home of Mr. and Mrs. Villiams who lived two houses down from my family. Both of them took a liking to me and at one time wanted to adopt me. Mom and Dad objected, but they would permit my going places with them. Most of our outings were to church.

On Wednesdays, Mrs. Villiams would go to a prayer meeting and Mr. Villiams and I would get together to bake cakes. I got pleasure out of flouring the cake pans, then we would sit around and talk about different things. One evening when I arrived all ready to work with the cake pans, to my disappointment, they had already been floured. I stood listening to Mrs. Villiams as she exited the door.

"Helmore has other plans for tonight. Take a seat in the dining room and wait. He'll be down soon. Bye now!" But just before the door shut, she yelled loud enough for her voice to carry upstairs. "Helmore, Sylvia is here. See you later, about nine." Her ride had arrived. She shut the door and was gone.

In the next two hours, I would learn more than any eight-year-old should learn.

"Sorry I took so long, but I was thinking about what you and I could do together tonight. Let's go into the living room and talk about some things."

He had already picked me up and was headed toward the front door, pulling down the shades, which was unusual. We sat in the big chair in the living room, me in Mr. Villiams's lap. This was not uncommon, as I had often sat with him in this manner before. But this night turned out differently than all other Wednesday nights. As we continued to talk, I noticed movement in Mr. Villiams's crotch. Looking at it, I was startled. After all, I was only eight years old! He took my hands and placed them on his erection. I was curious and didn't know what was moving up and down in his pants—as a moist spot now appeared making it look as he had wet himself. What did I know? I was a little girl!

"What are you doing, wetting your pants?" I asked as we both laughed.

He then pulled down his zipper and dug into his pants, pulling out what looked to me like a piece of flesh, not unlike an oversized worm, I remember thinking. With him holding my hands, he forced it back into his pants. Feeling it move and protrude, he then asked, "Do you want to see it?"

Still not completely exposed, I tried to pull back, screeching at the same time, "I don't want to feel that! Let me go home, now!" At only eight, I knew this wasn't right.

Mr. Villiams was no longer the nice man I knew at church. He was trying to kiss me with that Doublemint gum lodged in his mouth. He had the advantage over my little body. He then lay me down on the floor and forced himself up to my privates, but I gripped my legs tight as he forced me to open them.

"Hold still!" he said. When he realized I wasn't going to let him, he just rubbed up and down my private area until he'd ejaculated. *Of course, I didn't know what had happened, only that a creamy substance had emerged onto his pants.* I hated that odor along with his gyrations and sweat.

On my way home I thought, *Who can I tell this to?* I would have told my mother, but she was too busy looking after my cousin who had injured herself on a boy's bike. Maybe it was then that I started being secretive about a lot of situations which arose in my life.

A few days later we were playing, "Red Rover, Red Rover." I ran and hit the line of my opponents and up in the air I went landing my head on the pavement—I was knocked unconscious. I soon came to and looked up into the faces of the kids. They were laughing at me.

"That's not funny at all, you guys! I was out like a light!" When I said that, my friends laughed even harder.

Looking across at the familiar house for a moment, I was wondering if Mrs. Villiams saw what happened since we were close to her home. Maybe she could attest to the fact the boys and girls were playing a little too rough. Then, on second thought, I had pledged I would never go over to that house again. From that time on, I proposed in my heart to stay away from the Villiams's, and I did until years later, after I became *saved*. It was then that I would drive Sandy, Mr. Villiams's wife to Butler, Pennsylvania to visit her husband laying on his death bed at the Veterans Hospital. With a spirit of forgiveness, I prayed asking God to forgive the sins and heal him. Mr. Villiams died, as did his wife one year later.

Who cared what I was. I had been abused and what difference would it make to me—I was ruined. My Uncle Harry called me a woman, but to others I was a whore. Jesus called me "Sylvia." Others called me dirty, unfit names—not anything good. All I knew was, I was going to be a mother and didn't even know what it was all about. I would need a job and had only a seventh grade education, no experience of work other than in my home. How did Robert escape his responsibility? Keeping me from jumping off a bridge was the only help he gave. This baby would have been cared for after birth. How I managed once again, only God knows. How could he impregnate me and not take on his fatherly duties? How could he drive around knowing I would soon have his baby?

A premature baby at that, which didn't make it any easier for me. Two months after my operation, I was hospitalized for yet another illness when my kidneys gave me trouble. The night before I was discharged, I became really sick and had a great deal of pain. The doctor was called to my room to examine me—he mistreated me badly saying I was acting out and a lot of other nasty comments. Perhaps he was upset over my pregnancy, being an unwed mother and all. I don't know what it was, but he really hurt my feelings. After all, the doctor who had taken out my appendix didn't treat me like this.

The next morning, a nurse came into my room and told me to get ready to go home. "You're out of here today, my dear, whether you feel good or not. You were something bad last night and I won't tolerate people like you, nor your behavior, you b—.

If I knew what a dog's name meant at that time, maybe I would have knocked fire out of her. I was soon taken down the hall to talk with the doctor and my parents. There was no sympathy—from anyone. So many people had degraded me so badly that I eventually began to believe that I wasn't worth another day on this earth. Earlier at noon just before I was to go home I was given lunch while my parents finished the talk with my doctor.

Mom and Dad entered the room. "It's time to go home!"

I then began to vomit up my lunch. They thought that, too, was an act and that I was acting out. There were serious moments of silence as we passed down the hall on our way out of the hospital. Not one good word of advice, other than from my father.

"You think you can go home and behave yourself accordingly? I'm two minutes away from hurting you and I won't tolerate another moment!"

I couldn't believe I was being treated this way. What had I done to deserve this?

At home, I was told to go right upstairs to my bed, to the room I shared with my sister, Marva. Etta, my best friend, had come over to visit. She and I talked, but I had to keep using a bucket that had been put upstairs for me for convenience, since the bathroom was down in the basement. As I sat with my legs crossed, I noticed a clear fluid seeping from me. Little did I know, my water bag had broken. Etta noticed it, too.

"Girl, what are you doing? Can't you hold your water?"

We were both so naive.

"What is wrong with you? I'm going to go tell your mother to come see about this."

As I moved from the wet spot, I could see bloodstains. Etta noticed it too.

"Etta, I can feel the baby's head, right here!" I said as I touched myself.

Then Etta really panicked and ran for my mother, calling, "Mrs. Wilson, Sylvia is bleeding and she feels the baby's head!"

My mother came rushing into the room and looked at me. "How long has this been going on?"

"Since this morning, and the fluid has been coming out since lunch time. I just felt the head a few minutes ago."

Mom ran down to call the doctor. Then she yelled up the stairs for me to get ready to go back to the hospital as soon as Ralph, my brother-in-law, came. My father had gone to work. I was in labor and had been in labor all this time. It was 9:00 P.M. when my ride came, and I remember feeling the pressure of the baby's head as we drove toward the hospital.

Marvin was born two months premature on March 27, 1958. I never had any labor pains—the night I had been accused of acting out.

There was no pain up to the delivery, which was soon after we arrived at the hospital. Marvin weighed less than three pounds and had to stay in the hospital until he weighed at least five pounds before being allowed to come home. This gave me time to get plenty of rest, because I now had a heart ailment, too.

After I'd recuperated at home, I still was not able to go places, and of course, no one wanted me around them, not after just having a baby. My life was contaminated—at least to them it was.

Aunt Queen, Uncle Harry's wife was the first person to teach me a skill in order to earn money to care for my baby. Housecleaning would be the work I would apply for after her training. Eight dollars a day for working eight hours. Hey, that was better than nothing! I didn't earn much because I only worked one or two days a week. Mom and Dad took up the slack and I worked to take care of my baby, Marvin.

Marvin was named after my older sister, Marva. I remember the day he came home, a neighbor from up the street, came over to see my son.

"Is Robert the father of this baby? He don't look like him. He sure is ugly." She turned and walked away and never returned again.

I didn't say a word to her or anyone like her, just looked at their ignorance. We survived criticism. After all, they were only words.

After two months of having Marvin home, I adjusted to having a baby as part of my life. At nights when the baby would wake for a feeding, I would find my child on the floor, wrapped in a blanket I used to keep us warm while feeding. One morning he was not to be found as I looked through the blankets.

"Mom, did you see where my baby went?" Looking into her room, I could see my son in her arms.

"He's not lost, that's for sure. I took him out of your arms early this morning. You fell asleep feeding him. It's dangerous for you to sleep trying to feed your baby, so I'll keep him at night—if it's okay with you."

But that did not let me have one bit of freedom. Mom kept me close to the house, as if I were a wild ass on the loose. Sometimes at work, I found a bit of leisure time. I had no friends to visit now, not even my best friend, nor could I go anywhere—I only worked and cared for the baby. If I did go anywhere, I took my child with me, otherwise I stayed at home.

June had arrived and the boys and girls were getting out of school for the summer. My brother's classmate was leaving to join the Navy. A going-away party had been planned and all the neighborhood kids were going to be there. My brother felt sorry for me.

"Mom, let Sylvia go to this party. I'll make sure she stays in line. It's just down the block and you can see the house from the back door."

Mom consented and I rushed upstairs and got ready to go to Peewee's going-away party two blocks away. Free at last. Thank God, I was free! I was so happy I would be with old friends again. A few things ran through my mind, but I pushed them aside. I would see people I enjoyed. Who cared now whether they liked me or not— just to be away from the house was such a relief!

The party was going strong when I arrived. I adjusted to seeing the faces of my age group. For a while, I just sat looking on, maybe as if to see what the people thought of me being in their presence. They paid me no attention. They were too busy with the dancing and socializing with each other. Some totally ignored me and some said I should just relax and have a good time.

This young man whom I had seen many times at Reed's Arena, Jerome came in with his crowd as I was slow dancing with Willie. I could see him talking to my schoolmates, Vern and my best friend Etta in the next room. Soon he came over and asked me to dance with him. I felt like I couldn't dance a fast dance yet, so we waited for the next slow one.

"You look good, girl. Tell me, did you marry the baby's father? You know I always liked you and we could have had a lot of fun together. I wanted you to be my lady." He continued. "Look, there's another party down the street. Come and go with me and the gang. Bring your girlfriends, too, okay?"

I pondered the question. "I must ask my brother first. You go and see what he might say."

He returned from seeing my brother and told me I could go, only I had to take my girlfriends with me. Billyboy did walk over to confirm it was okay, but said I should make it back before he got home. We all agreed and I walked out to the porch and waited until everyone was together. It had started to rain and we all hesitated for a moment. The car was across the street in front of us. The fellows ran over first, then we girls followed. We ran fast to the car, stopping at the door which had been opened for us. I was the last one to reach the vehicle, but was pushed by the girls and pulled into the car by the boys. The car pulled away from the curb leaving my girlfriends standing behind with puzzled looks on their faces. I had no idea what was happening, but I knew something was wrong. Terribly wrong.

I started to argue with the boys inside the car before the vehicle reached the next block at Overland and Myrtle Street.

"What are you going to do?"

Then Jimmy's hands were all over me.

"Jimmy, get your hands off me! I can't go with you guys, alone. Jimmy, get your dirty nails off my flesh! Hey, the girls!" I pleaded.

The boys just laughed.

"You boys are in for trouble if you lay one hand on me." I was about to be raped and nothing could stop them. The driver, Jerome, who'd made all the plans, drove while the others took their turns with me. Jimmy was mean and held me down as I fought to keep Clyde, who was first in line, off me. When he was through, it was the next guy's turn, and after that, Jerome. By now, I'd stopped fighting them. It was pointless and I knew that if I struggled, it would only make things worse.

"Man, stop and take the wheel over! We don't want to kill her," Jerome said.

Jimmy moved to the front and took the wheel while Jerome climbed over to the backseat.

"Okay girl, it's my turn and I ain't gonna hurt you. Now let's do it right." By now I was so worn out from the struggle that I couldn't even feel anything as he penetrated me. My legs and thighs felt numb. My hair had turned nappy, my clothes were wrinkled, and I smelled something awful.

Now standing in front of the house where I should have been in the first place, I saw that everyone was gone, so I started walking home alone. *Alive,* I thought, *but what do I do? Someone, please help me!* I then heard a voice.

"Go home!" It was soft, gentle, seemingly in my mind, but it wasn't.

"Go home?" I responded, "Whoever you are, I'm in great trouble."

Once again I was listening to the same voice I had heard hundreds of times before.

I entered the basement door to find the house was quiet. I went to the bathroom which was in the back down in the basement. Sitting on the commode, I could hear everything being said upstairs. I yelled as I checked myself out.

"Right here, Bill, in the basement!"

I heard Mom say she hadn't heard me come in and that the baby was crying upstairs.

"Oh, I've been, uhh…in the house and getting a few clean clothes for Marvin." *Lying won't get you anywhere,* I thought.

I put that night far out of my mind—who would believe me anyhow? Molested, raped, and now gang raped…

My days returned to normal. I cleaned and worked with Aunt Queen or just sat at the kitchen window by our phone, then one night, Brandon called.

"I'll be home for your sixteenth birthday, Syl. I'll ask your mother when I return home if we can go to the drive-in on the east side. We won't go alone—another couple will go, too, so it won't look suspicious. See you soon. Love you. Bye."

Brandon came and did just as he said he would. His dad let him use his car and we drove to the Skyline Drive-in Theater on the east side off Route 422. We put the speaker onto our window and began to watch the movie. Midway through, Brandon asked me to sit a little closer to him. I was close, but he wanted to make it clear what was about to happen and he needed my ears closer to his lips as he spoke.

"I want to have sex with you tonight and don't want you to say no. I will marry you as soon as I put a few months in the service. Will you marry me?" He pulled out a friendship ring and placed it on my finger.

"Yes," I said, but let's leave the sex out."

Brandon and I spent time together and we eventually got involved and he promised that if I became pregnant, he would see to it we got married.

21

Pregnant I was, and scared, too. I had hoped it was a delay because of some new ailment, but no. I could feel that little knot forming in my belly. I even sat Marvin on that area of my stomach and could feel the throbbing. There was life once again forming, waiting to develop, to enter this world. Now how in the world was I going to get out of this? This is a situation I had full control of, and was truly my fault. My mother had threatened to put me in a girl's home before she'd go through that embarrassment again.

When Brandon finally called, I told him I was pregnant. He got in touch with my mother and his mother and they started planning a wedding right away. My parents had given me a choice. Get married or go to a girl's home. Not knowing what went on in one of those homes, I said, "Okay, I'll marry."

As plans were being made, Brandon got into some kind of trouble with the military. He had beat a man with a trench shovel, nearly killing him, and at his hearing he was found guilty. The wedding plans continued, and unfortunately I was not aware of his crime until long after our marriage. It wouldn't be until the marriage ceremony that I knew something had actually happened.

It was now February. My wedding gown Mom made herself, was packed, and we—that is, Brandon's parents and mine—all headed to Ft. Meade, Maryland, outside Washington, D.C. I sat looking out at the clear, cold night, listening to the conversation in the car. My mind was distant and I tried to communicate with that soft voice which seemed to be there when I needed it, but nothing, just movement in the stars deep in the sky. *What will tomorrow bring me*, I thought.

The next morning arrived. The big wedding day. It was very cold, about three degrees above zero, and the coat I was wearing was loaned to me by my sister Marva. I remember how Ralph, my brother in law, came to the house the day Marva graduated.

"Mrs. Wilson, I've come to take my wife home," Ralph said. "Now that she is out of school and we've been married since January, she can live with me in the apartment close by here."

It was her suit coat she had married Ralph in that now kept me warm.

The church was on military grounds. It was white and very small and it was here in which services were held for those in the Army. We all went in and took a seat. An usher came over and Mr. Lee,

Brandon's father, stated our reason for being there. The usher left and soon the preacher came out in his Army uniform.

"Today there will be a wedding ceremony. Sylvia, will you come forth and stand here. Who is standing with you?" the preacher asked.

"I have no one," I replied.

The preacher looked out over his congregation and appointed a foreign girl to come stand as my maid of honor. We waited for Brandon to arrive. It was a few minutes which seemed like hours when he finally walked into the little chapel, but he wasn't alone. He had two officers by his side—and Brandon's wrists were handcuffed, and shackles hugged his ankles. The officers were asked by the minister to remove the handcuffs, which they did, but his feet remained chained together. We hurriedly said our wedding vows, kissed, and were given only a few minutes to talk. Brandon did most of the talking, but never gave me a reason why he had to shuffle into the church like that. My heart was broken seeing him like this, for our wedding, and later when I asked what was going on, he hushed me up.

"Sylvia, let's talk about tomorrow. I only have a few minutes with you and I want to know what your plans are. I'll be fine and I may have to do some time. Wait for me, okay. You'll hear about it later." He kissed me on my forehead, then was taken away.

The wedding was behind me as we prepared and journeyed back home, not stopping for anything, not even supper. As we drove back, I felt that maybe with this baby on the way, now that I was married, I could gain a little respect and be treated better. February 3, 1959, was our wedding date.

On February 17th, two weeks later, I went into labor and delivered Nelson weighing in at four pounds, six ounces. I had heart failure during the delivery and when I came to, awakening in my room, with IV fluids dripping into the veins of my arms, and oxygen prongs up my nose, I was told I'd barely made it. A rheumatic heart condition from having strep throat when I was younger was what brought the problem on.

Respect was far from me when my mother asked, "Sylvia, have you been with someone other than Brandon? Did you make a mistake about who fathered the baby?" Her voice faded away as I passed in and out of consciousness. The next day my mother-in-law visited.

She, too, asked the same questions. I was eager to hear and understand, yet still confused by all these questions.

"What is wrong? Is something the matter with my baby?"

She, seeing how upset I was, just patted my hands. "I will be back when you feel better. Just tell me, who is the baby's father? It's surely not my son, Brandon."

As she walked out of the room, my mind pondered. *Hey, where are my flowers? My gifts, my congratulations, or even a get-well card! Isn't that how it's supposed to be?*

Chapter 5

Reflecting on my young life, I would say I had some good days, but there were the bad, too. They seemed to balance out so when I had my good days, look out, for the bad would soon come from around the corner, just like clockwork—but who was working my clock?

For instance, at school while in gym class, playing one of my favorite activities, I fell down, ruining the game for my other classmates.

"Get up!" my teacher hollered, pulling me to the side like a rag doll, slamming me up against the gymnasium wall. "You won't be playing any more this quarter until you straighten your act up. Go home and bring your parents back to school with you."

She kept pulling at me to stand up, but I really couldn't. The bell rang. The teacher left me there, and it was a while before I got my strength to stand up and go home—and when I arrived there, Mom and Dad had a few friends over playing cards. I didn't say a thing, just got on the couch and fell asleep. I could hear a voice call out.

"Sylvia, get up, it's time for the second bell! Hurry, get up now, you're going to be late! Sylvia, get up!"

It was my mother trying to stir me so I could get back to school. Getting to school on time meant a lot and when I heard my uncle, my mother's brother, say, "You're going to be late!" I jumped to my feet and cut out like a light, running as fast as my little legs could go. As I ran up the street and headed across the short path which would bring me right in front of the school, I fell. I tried to get up, but I couldn't. A man working on his car saw me trying to stand. He picked me up.

"Where do you live?" he asked.

"Cleveland Street," was my quiet answer.

He then headed toward my home.

"Your daughter fell crossing the path and was struggling to get up. When I went over to help, I realized she couldn't move, so I brought her to you." He laid me on the couch.

I didn't know what was going to happen next. Mom and Dad weren't rich; they couldn't afford to incur bills of any sort. I guess I cost them lots of money and heartaches, too. I laid there, it seemed for weeks, before I was taken to the hospital. I was finally placed in a long dark hall, too weak to remember much of anything that happened after that. I do, however, remember being placed in the children's ward a few days later.

During my stay in the hospital it was discovered I had a disease found mostly in African-American people called Sickle Cell Anemia. It's said to be passed on to children by their parents. It's a hereditary blood disorder—one parent carries the "S" trait and the other carries the "C" trait. This is called S.C. Hemoglobin Disease.

How I managed with this disease, only God knows. I put away trying to reason when in a crisis. Joint pain and dehydration were just a few of its many symptoms. I had to get plenty of fluids and rest. Colds, a sore throat, any infection could bring on a crisis. Even if I were to swim during the summer and catch a chill, would bring me down fast. It starts with stomachaches, then my whole body's filled with pain. Blankets, water, and pain pills are my history—and, of course, lots of hospitalization.

Watching the blood drip from a bottle into my veins brought back more memories of the ups and downs in my life. The day I was discharged from the hospital, my younger sister Connie was being admitted with the same diagnosis. She and my younger brothers were found to have Sickle Cell Anemia, too. It's not contagious. How my mother and dad managed with four children suffering at one time or another, I still wonder.

Things went on as usual. Every summer, usually in August, I went through agony, always having a crisis it seemed. I learned I could not be hospitalized each time I had an illness. Dehydration, then blood coagulating and starving the main organs from their proper intake of oxygen for them to function properly, caused excruciating pain. It was like someone cutting me in half with a knife. If the pain settled in my legs, I would get a pair of crutches and hop about playing. If it was in my arms, I would wear a sling to tolerate the pain just to be able to go outside and play with the neighborhood kids. I was called a hypochondriac and a big put-on, and knowing how people are, lots of other things. But I learned that sticks and stones may hurt my bones—along with the pain—but words would never hurt me. I also learned how to live alone, which I hated. But during my illness, people would wear me out when visiting. I had more than my share of sickness and would have been glad to share some of those days. I thank God that He was with me to bear it all. I know I couldn't have made it without Him.

Days passed before my doctor permitted me out of bed to go see my baby for the first time. Nine days to be exact. I was pushed to the nursery by a nice nurse. I sat in my wheelchair looking through the big glass window at all the babies, the nurse standing by my side. I tried to locate my son.

"Do you see him? Look over there, in the corner. He looks like you!"

The nurse on the other side of the glass walked over to the window and shook her head.

"No, that's not your baby. When did you deliver?"

Another nurse said, "Look," she said pointing toward a dark-skinned baby in an incubator with tubes connected to his head and arms. "That's your baby!"

He looked so listless, and not at all like me.

"That's not my baby!" I said as they pushed him up to the window for me to see.

"Oh yes, this is the baby you had a few days back. I helped deliver him. Isn't he precious?"

The nurse was so positive, then I began to remember that horrible night I must have conceived this baby. The night of the rape in the car with those awful boys. I thought back to the last one—Jerome, the driver. It had to be his. The baby looked just like him. Black as night...

There were all those questions my mother and mother-in-law had interrogated me with some days ago. So this was why no flowers! I fainted. Maybe the nurse thought I was having a relapse, so she took me right back to my room and hooked me back to another I.V.

Later as I was laying in bed, my mother came in to the room.

"Mom, did you see the baby? I did!"

She had taken a chair and pulled it close to the bed.

"No, but I want to talk with you about your mother-in-law," she said with concern across her face. "No way is that baby her son's—you been around with some other man! Now tell me and don't tell a lie."

"Mom, I need to talk to my husband."

27

I was confused. Why hadn't my mother seen the baby yet? She had met Brandon's mother on her way to see the baby, but they had a few words, causing my mother to leave without seeing my son. With both the baby and I in serious condition, she waited until she calmed down before seeing Nelson.

Mom left the room to see the baby while the nurse started up another blood transfusion. As I watched the blood drip, my mind wandered back to the awful night—the night of the rape. But who was it? I then saw the driver, the last to calmly approach me. This was now my punishment. *Oh God, can you help me now?*

Mom was back in the room. "Sylvia, that's not Brandon's child. Whose is it and don't lie!"

I just looked at her and said, "I'm not sure. I'll tell you when I get home."

She turned with disgust and left.

Why didn't I die a few days ago? It had to have been the driver's, Jerome—he was the last person who...

Why this agony, why not die? I recalled just before my wedding I had been hospitalized with the rheumatic heart ailment. I was placed in a room across from the nurse's station for them to keep an eye on me. While I slept, I had a dream. I saw God standing on a pinnacle talking to the crowd of people.

"Go to the upper room and be saved."

He fell into the crowd and broke up into pieces. His flesh began to crack apart like clay breaking, then blood flowed and the blood turned into water which flowed between our feet. All of us standing in the crowd ran toward the upper room. I was a part of that crowd and pushed my way up until I stood in the designated room. The water rose to my chin and I awoke out of that dream. And that's when I saw Jesus! He had been standing near my bed, then diminished into the cross which hung on the wall in front of me, there in my room. A nurse ran in to see if I needed assistance. I had been seriously ill with a rheumatic fever ailment and was threatening to abort my pregnancy. The nurse finished working with the tubing in my vein as I told her about my dream. She then walked out and the cleaning lady came over to my bedside.

"Could you let me tell you what you saw in your dream? I heard you telling the nurse." Looking steadfastly at me, she spoke. "You'll see salvation. You will be a special person. God is going to use you, you'll see, honey!" As the nurse returned, the cleaning lady kept saying, "You will see!"

The nurse said, "See what?"

I repeated the dream, saying, "And I saw Jesus vanish into the cross." She, like so many others, showed little concern until I refused to say another word about it. It sounded so far-fetched, I felt like I was lying. I just clamed up. As for death, it was not my time—only I felt it was a way of escape.

Soon that was all behind me and I went to live with my grandfather who lived next door to my parents. I could not continue living with my parents because there was too much tension, ill feelings, and hatred. My father was very cruel and fought with me at the drop of a hat. My mother held off the beatings as much as she could. With Grandpa next door living alone, we talked it over and I took the front bedroom in his house to help clean and cook.

Brandon's mother persuaded him to file for a divorce. She was not going to let her son stay in a marriage knowing the baby wasn't his. She instructed her son to stay out of or get as far from our relationship we'd built together. I talked to him and he told me not to say or do anything until he came home from serving out his prison time in Fort Leavenworth, Kansas. He also told me not to get upset, because his mother was rightly concerned. Brandon never shared with his parents that he knew he had not fathered my child. I told him all about the rape at the drive-in theater. He asked me not to make mention of it ever again and said he would take care of the matter. This he did. He kept his word and carried out the promise.

Brandon came home after eighteen months had passed. I recall the night he and his dad pulled up in front of my house. I had been sitting on the neighbor's steps when I noticed the light green Pontiac slowly pull up, stopping in front of my house. I jumped with joy.

"Hey that's my…!"

I stopped and ran a few feet, then walked. Brandon stepped out of the car. He was on business and we just walked up and entered the house.

"Can I see the baby? Where is he?"

I went up to the bedroom, passing Grandpa who sat near the stairway door. When I came down with Nelson in my arms, Grandpa got up to leave Brandon and I alone with Nelson. I placed Nelson in Brandon's arms.

"Sylvia, did you tell the father about his son?" I thought it was funny he asked.

"Yes, he was here just two nights ago and saw his baby. We talked and agreed he had fathered this child." I continued to try and explain all the baby's father and I had talked about. One thing Jerome couldn't understand was why I never said anything to him about the pregnancy. Well, at first I heard he was married or in jail, and also I didn't know where he lived. But the main reason was, I had put it all out of my mind. I also told Brandon, "I had to, in my mind, forgive those boys in the car for what wrong they did to me. Remember, Brandon, you helped when you told me if I was pregnant, you would marry me."

With the threat of divorce, Brandon and I just kept our distance until one night when I was out of the Ritz Bar. I was unaware Brandon and his lawyer sat across from me as I sipped from a glass of beer. It wasn't until a drink was sent my way that I noticed them. I gave a smile and nodded my head.

"Thank you!"

Soon there he was, standing next to me, asking for a dance.

"Yes, what harm can it do?"

We slow danced and for the first time, my head rested on his chest. I felt his heart rhythm in my ears as it beat with contentment. His lawyer walked over and tapped Brandon on the shoulder.

"Man, you might as well forget the divorce, I'll deal with your mother myself."

That night I lay and thought about Brandon and how warm he felt there in the club. Then I heard a tap on the front window. Pulling the curtains back, to my surprise, it was Brandon.

"Hurry, let me in!"

I hesitated until he said, "Open this window and let your husband in. We are married!"

For a few weeks, the window was his way to see me. Then he made up his mind to save the marriage and started to use the front door.

We did fine for a little while. Everyone felt good about us staying together. After all, we were married, so it was best to work out our relationship. Brandon invited his sister Nola over for supper one evening. She and my Uncle John joined us and we ate and played cards. By the time we were finished it was late and so we all decided to bunk up—the boys with the boys, and the girls with the girls.

Tired, I had gone ahead to see after my children and then got into bed. Half-asleep, I could just hear when Lynola climbed into bed and lay beside me. I was nearly asleep when I felt her hands rubbing up and down my thighs. I moved her hands over and turned to get comfortable, when a sound came from her—a lustful sound. I sat up. My first impression was maybe she's sleeping and unaware of what she was doing.

"Brandon, come get your sister out of my bed, now! Right now! Girl, get up and go home," I told her. "Brandon, take her out of here, like real quick!"

Her mouth was so foul, as if I had done something to her. She angrily grabbed her clothes.

"I'm not coming over to your house again, not ever. You'll regret this!"

She turned to her brother and then attacked him.

"Man, you told me she was up to those happenings! You better hip her to how it really is, wake her up to life!"

Pushing past him, she snapped, "I can help myself out, I don't need your help!" She then ran down the stairs screaming more filthy words.

While I rested, I let my mind go over what had taken place. Where had I gone wrong? She and my uncle had been in prison at one time or another, but never would I involve myself rubbing up against another woman. It's just not my style. Our communication broke that night. One last encounter with her was that she fired her gun at me, as we fled her apartment. Brandon's mother and I had gone to tell her about a death in the family.

The tension just kept building until one afternoon while the family sat at the lunch table eating, and Marvin would not eat his food, Brandon, playing the father role, began to force food into his mouth. I, at first did not say a word. I didn't want my husband to feel he had no right to correct his now adopted son. When Marvin resisted, Brandon took a strap which hung over a chair, and hit him across the head, hard. I grabbed a Coke bottle and with my eyes closed, swung it toward Brandon, hitting above his left eye. When I looked, blood was streaming down his face.

My screams, my shouts, and the children crying brought my Uncle Bob into the house to see what was the matter. He immediately took hold of Brandon's hand, who was about to hit me.

"Come on, man. You got to go take care of this. I'll drive you to the hospital." As he left the house with my uncle, he stopped.

"Sylvia, please forget what you did. I forgive you, okay, honey? See you when I get back!"

He was making sure it was all right to return. When I agreed to all he was saying, he opened the door, turned for a second, and said, "I'll take care of you later."

Decent jobs were hard to find outside the steel mills in Youngstown. Brandon got work at the Towel Supply, which paid very little weekly. I worked cleaning homes when I could find work. How we made it, God only knows. There were times my Uncle John and Brandon went out to steal so we could have a meal on our table. Many times we ate what Grandpa fixed. But when we were talked about, how broke as all get out we were, Grandpa, or Pa as we would call him, would not hesitate to feed us and this made family members mad. We decided to try other ways.

Other ways meant I had to go out on the street and sell my little body to the whore-mongers. Where did I get such an idea? My husband planted that thought. He told me how to go about standing on the street corners until a man pulled up and asked for a "trick." He didn't force me to do it at first, and it took wondering where the next meal would come from before I decided to try this. We didn't have food, and we were hungry and too proud to beg.

My first try, I went and stood on the corner of Hillman and Cleveland Street near the bus stop. It was about nine o'clock when I reached the area. I hadn't had a chance to change my mind before a man pulled up.

"Get in!" He didn't even ask for a trick, just said "Get in!"

He drove off talking.

"What is your reason for getting in this car? I hope it's not to prostitute."

The word *prostitute* at that time was unknown to me and I had no understanding of what he meant.

"Oh, I was told by my husband to stand on the corner and wait for a man to pull up and offer me some money for a trick."

The man pulled out a badge and said, "I can put you under arrest for this!"

That detective drove me downtown to the east side where we sat and watched girls wave men down and drive off. I learned a lot from this man that night. Before I got out of his car, he put a fifty dollar bill in my hands and told me he had better not catch me on the street again.

It was weeks before I tried again, but now I had to see for myself how it really worked. I wouldn't go for any other reason, just because I was curious. All dressed up, I reached the corner and to my surprise, a man pulled and asked for a trick.

"I got twenty dollars."

I got in not knowing where to go or what to do. We drove down near the park under a bridge, and reaching in his pants, he told me what to do with my mouth. He then grabbed my head. *Oh God*, I thought, *is this what I have to do for money?* I gagged because he stunk. Bright lights soon flooded the area as a man approached the car. It was the detective—he had followed the car.

"Go get into my car and I'll handle this man!"

Once in the car, we drove around and I got the biggest lecture about what could happen to me, about the chances I was taking, and how I could lose my babies. He then took me to a house.

"You can work in a clean area where the men are checked and the money is good. The street is too dangerous."

After seeing the place, he drove me back home, but this time he didn't offer any money, only advice.

"Stay out of the streets!"

I never told my husband what I learned and it was months before I would try it again.

It was now 1962 and we soon moved into the Westlake Projects on the north side of town. Brandon and I managed his pay as best as we knew. On the weekends we would go out to friends' homes and play cards or go down to a place near the railroad tracks and get a pitcher of beer for seventy-five cents, enjoying the crowd that gathered. One night we went to the Silver Dollar on the east end to have a few drinks, after which, Brandon started acting crazy. Outside as we started walking toward home, I kept hearing him say ugly things.

"Hey, girl, go turn a trick. We need some money."

He would then pull my dress up and yell out loud "Want a trick? Here she is! Come on, man!"

He then pulled me out into the street, causing the heel of my shoe to break off. The scene was bad and I felt awful. Whatever got into him I don't know, but I realized his responsibilities were too much. Twenty-eight dollars a week wasn't enough for the four of us to make it. The pressures got worse and so did my husband. He fought with me and hit my babies. One day I came home from downtown and caught Brandon immersing my boys into scalding hot water. I tried to report this behavior to the police, but they never came to my rescue. Now I was forced to hit the streets and bring home money or get beaten up. I went over to the house the detective took me, where it was clean, more like a job. After a time, the "job" enabled us to purchase our first car.

The job as a call girl was far better than taking chances going from car to car with strangers. The men who came for *service* were checked for venereal disease. The house man did it, or we girls were shown how to detect a venereal disease. Our first duty was to wash and look for a problem. Men were only allowed a limited amount of time in the room with the girls. He could pay for as many girls as he desired, but was still allotted time with each of them. The house man would knock on the door.

"Time is up! Come on out now or pay up!"

Most of the men were so turned on that while they were being examined, they would prematurely *finish their business*, which made our jobs easy. Of course when a man came in with a bad attitude and started some mess, the house man would put him out.

I only worked for a few weekends before I got sick of the place. I did not want to involve myself with the games after work because they took away the ease of working. One night my friend Kim and I arrived to work and got ourselves ready, putting on our sheer evening gowns, as did some of the college girls who came to work in order to pay for their tuition. Dressed in our negligees, we waited for some customers.

"Leave this place," I heard someone say.

I turned to Kim. "Let's go home tonight. I don't feel right about tonight."

She refused. I got up and excused myself for the night. I even told the house man something wasn't like it should be, but I couldn't put my finger on the problem. I left. I was just a block away and I decided maybe I should go back. So I turned around and that's when I saw the house surrounded by police, and everyone was being put into the paddy wagon, which took them to the city jail.

Kim accused me of ratting, but I never even thought of such a thing. Maybe if I had to tell anything, it would be how the house man and his wife coerced the girls into having sex parties with them. I couldn't go along with that can of worms. That night I proposed in my heart to tell Brandon all his beatings and his coercing me into doing despicable things for money, were over. I never told him it was that voice within which told me to leave that place. Or was it the love of my children? Kim and I remained friends, but we lost trust in each other.

One night while out with my husband, we left the place by the railroad tracks and headed home. A car pulled up and it was my old-time friend Bar's husband Willie, who asked if I had seen her. Both Brandon and I stopped to listen, but when I turned to walk on with my husband, he had gone ahead. I wondered what was the matter. Was he mad? I kept walking, hoping to see him, but my husband had disappeared. Then just as quickly, I saw a silhouette. My husband came out of the dark, but before I could say a word, he knocked me out. I awoke to him kicking and dragging me down the walkway to our front steps where he banged my head on the concrete and steel steps, until I was unconscious. Death should have taken me then.

At the hospital I was strapped to a stretcher. Brandon done a real good job on me. He carried my nearly unconscious body to St. Elizabeth Hospital, where they got in touch with my parents. My mother sat and begged me to press charges. "I won't, Mom." With my broken ribs and battered head, I went home to heal and look after my children. They were in just as much danger, so I went home to care for them. What had I done? Maybe I deserved what I got? So we would just give our marriage another go.

Promises were made by Brandon to me and my children that he would no longer harm us. For a while we lived a pretty normal life.

Friends came to our apartment and we would often visit other homes playing card games. We sat for hours eating, laughing, and just having fun.

I soon became pregnant again. On one occasion, for some reason or another, I decided to walk home after visiting the Dubois home. As I walked down the middle of Wirt Street, I failed to notice the ice under the snow tire tracks. I slipped and took a hard fall, right on the baby in my belly. When I reached my apartment, I felt faint and saw blood flowing down my legs into my boot. I felt a great deal of pressure in my lower abdomen, so I sat down to catch my breath—and to my shock, a mass gushed from me. It wasn't a pretty sight. I went into the bathroom and cleaned myself up and got over to the hospital as soon as I could. The doctors confirmed what I already knew. I had aborted the pregnancy. After the examination, I was told to see my doctor six weeks from that day. I didn't feel badly about the loss of that pregnancy, even though Brandon deserved a child of his own. It was God's intention. At the doctor's visit some months later, to my surprise, I learned I was still going to have a baby in a few months. I had been carrying twins and had aborted only one fetus. Twins run in our families.

Summer approached us fast that year in and I was pretty sick with this pregnancy. Toxemia kept me in and out of the hospital for those next few months. This gave my husband time to run wild. Days would pass and I lay trying to recuperate. More times than not, I saw him after Mom or someone else would bring me home from the hospital. I never questioned his whereabouts. Our town was not as large as one might think; it was pretty small when it came to knowing one's business. Brandon's business usually got back to me.

"I saw your husband and Kim hanging out strong last night. What happened to you?" And so on…

I just settled back and carried my baby in my belly the best I could. I didn't even let conversations worry me. Even with all the gossip about my husband and his affairs, it didn't take away the fact I was his wife. But what did trouble me was, one night while walking home, we got into a spat. Brandon pushed me down and jumped on my stomach, repeatedly yelling.

"I don't want you or that bastard baby!" He kicked me over and over until I rolled up into a ball, then he stomped my back and thighs.

The bruises soon vanished. Not long after that fight, I lay waiting for Brandon to return home from one of his hanging out nights. It was middle of August, very hot and muggy. Hours had passed until early morning, when I heard him come in the apartment and climb the stairs. He walked to my bedside and stood looking at me, then got into his side of the bed. I lay still because I never knew his temperament. As soon as he came to bed, I rose up and went into the bathroom. A few minutes later, I came out of the bathroom and as I was making my way toward the bed, I was suddenly hit with a pain in my chest that literally took my breath away. I could not move nor talk, and my legs began to buckle out from under me. Brandon turned over to see what was happening. I was gasping for air and he jumped out of bed. Seeing me gasp for air, he jumped out of bed, and came to where I was nearly passing out. It felt as if a ton of bricks fell onto my chest. Without a word, Brandon picked me up, went down the stairs and out the front door, and ran toward the hospital.

"Hold on girl! Syl, you can't die on me now, not with all this ahead of us. Come on, hold on, girl! Don't give up! Hold on!"

Brandon kept on running towards the hospital and as he ran, he begged and asked me to forgive him and began to run harder to St. Elizabeth's Hospital. The emergency room was not far from our apartment, thank God!

When we reached the hospital, Brandon stood in front of the nurse's desk.

"My wife, my wife!" He stood holding my unclothed body with my bare behind hanging in the nurse's face.

"She's pregnant and is about to have the baby. Please help!"

The attendant came and placed me on a gurney. Without words, the white-coated men pushed me down the hall to an elevator, then rushed me up to the delivery floor. After placing me in a room to prep me for delivery, a doctor walked into examine me. With one look he yelled, breaking the glass on the medicine cabinet.

"This girl is in cardiac arrest! Hurry! She's not having a baby!"

A needle went into my upper arm, then the nurse and doctor moved quickly to assist. Soon I was moved to another area where nurses watched all night, praying while the nuns said the rosary. As I lay, I heard the Hail Marys repeated throughout that night. God was full of grace then. I was very sick up to the time a few weeks later when I delivered.

My son Lee was born September 27, 1962. He was a few months premature and weighed three pounds, eight ounces. Lee would stay in the nursery until he gained up to five pounds, before he could come home. With the birth of my son Lee, gave Brandon reason to seek employment out of state. A friend directed him to Ossinging, New York where he could stay with his family until he landed a job. I really had time to rest, with Lee still in the hospital, Marvin and Nelson with my mother, and Brandon gone. Thank God for my mother who saw after my children even after I joined Brandon in Ossinging. She kept them a few more months. Lee's premature birth left him underdeveloped. To train him was difficult. After testing Lee, it was recommended that he be put in a special school, but we moved so much, he never got a chance to attend.

Chapter 6

Ossinging, New York, was the place my husband had gone in order to find a real job which would enable us to maintain a standard of living. He called and made arrangements for me to join him. We would send for the children to come later when we both held a job. I sold what furniture I had and packed my belongings, gave my children over to my mother, and took a bus to New York to be with my husband.

About twenty miles up the Hudson River, Ossinging, New York, is about twenty miles up from the city of New York. It was guaranteed we would accomplish the task of finding real paying jobs, ones which would stabilize our living. I arrived by Greyhound bus, then took a train up the Hudson to the Ossinging train station where I got a cab to drive me to the address on the State Street a few blocks from Sing-Sing Prison. The people welcomed me with such warmth as they led me to my husband's room.

"He's been looking for you. What took you so long in coming?"

I never uttered a word, just followed the young lady down a flight of stairs to the basement and knocked at a door.

"Brandon, wake up, your wife is here! Go on in. He'll be glad to see you," she said as the door opened.

"Hi there. Wake up, it's your long-lost wife," I said, shaking him.

Brandon reached up and pulled me down with gladness in his eyes. It was as if we were to start a relationship all over again. It seemed the old saying may have been true— *"absence makes the heart grow fonder."*

My first job was with the Howard Johnson Motel Corporation outside of Tarrytown, New York. I worked hard and cleaned twenty-two rooms per day. One day I finished at two o'clock, two hours earlier than usual. I had skipped my lunch. My supervisor asked me to take the hour and a half to go over each room. I refused because I had already done my work. She fired me on the spot. I went home with my paycheck and made up my mind that sort of work was not for me.

The woman who lived on the second floor found me a position at the Grassland Hospital where I trained to be a nurse's aide. I held that job until I got sick. Brandon worked for a private firm as a guard and soon he was hired by the General Motors Corporation in Tarrytown, where we found an apartment and moved to White Street with only our clothing and used newspaper to sleep on. One day a man was fixing another apartment in the building and noticed our living conditions. He told my husband that evening he could help get our apartment filled with furniture from across the river. That weekend we had all the bedding, kitchen, and living room furniture we needed. We purchased our first refrigerator, stereo, and television on time. I was so grateful, and we worked and managed to gain good credit.

My next job would be cleaning homes, on-the-spot jobs. There was a company which sent you out if you sat and waited for a call to come through—with their recommendation. It was while I waited to be sent out that I met a man named Harold. He often came to help the ladies get from job to job. At first I took the bus, but one day he took me way out where there was no bus line. On the way home Harold told me he had put a bag of groceries at my back door and he knew I needed help. I told him my jobs were really helping and then thanked him for whatever he did. Harold knew more about my business than I did because he sat with the ladies, listening to the latest gossip. With this he began to pay a lot of attention to me when I came looking for work. One day he drove me to work out in Pleasantville, New York, and he talked about some things he had heard of my marriage. I wanted to hear more.

"I put those groceries at your back door. Did you get them, or did your husband throw out the food? Without waiting for an answer, Harold continued. "I've been waiting for this time to be alone with you. If you don't mind, I'll pick you up earlier to take you out to dinner."

That evening, after finding a babysitter right in the apartment building, we ate out at Howard Johnson's. Harold became my only friend.

With the boys now with us, I had to keep up my jobs and care for our home, plus be a wife. Brandon made being a wife easy as our current ability to begin to establish a standard of good living increased. But he was back to his old tricks, hanging out most of the time. He then began to be a part-time dad around the house and was part-time paying bills, too. I struggled to maintain the apartment and children. But Harold, my friend, helped a great deal when Brandon neglected his duties.

One night Brandon came home from being out late as usual. I had been playing with Lee and had just put him down beside me in my bed when Brandon came in and sat on top of me, beating my face severely. The next morning I put on my sunglasses and took a bus to Ellsford to work in a factory where I assembled plastic objects for Avon and other companies. When I got off the bus, a car followed me as I walked toward my job. I noticed a man behind the wheel. He pulled over and leaned out his window to speak to me.

"I know why you're wearing those sunglasses. That's what your husband did because of me. Want me to beat him up for you?"

I stopped and paid attention to what he was saying because I wanted to know why I was beat on last night.

"Pick me up from work this evening at three forty-five."

The man's name was Bobby Elton and when I got out of work, he was there waiting for me. I got in his car and we drove around while he told his story of how and why I got beat up on.

"You see, we were out at a club in Peekskill, New York. My sister was with your husband and I challenged him. I told him I would have you and that I would keep my mouth shut about his relationship with my sister. We made a deal, but he took it out on you. I saw you many times walking around town, and lady, you sure look good to me. Your husband came home and fought with you because of me. I'll deal with him, if you say so. I don't like him anyhow."

I got out of Bobby's car. "Thanks, but no thanks." I could not go along with anything he or Brandon were up to. When I walked off he kept moving along with me, yelling from his car window about things he could do for me to make me happy. At home I kept my mouth shut and went about my everyday duties. Weighing it all out to my advantage, this gave me reason to be with Harold without guilt.

One night on a date with Harold, he told of an accident he had years ago which had destroyed his sexual relationship with his wife. He told me he had a surprise to show me, and if I could help him feel good, I would never want for anything. We drove upstate to a motel. In the room, I sat on the bed as he handed me a box.

"Open it!" he said, pushing the box onto my lap.

"What is it?" The gadget looked like a man's sex organ. He asked me if he could put it on and make out with me.

"No!"

It was so funny, but I tried hard not to laugh in his face. He then strapped that ugly thing on his leg and started rubbing up and down my thighs.

"You see why my wife never let me use this on her?"

I felt so sorry for him, I welled up with tears, but I was so glad I didn't let him see me laughing, because this was a serious moment for Harold. We drove back and he told me about his life and the accident, how he had lost a lung and his male organs. He also mentioned he would soon retire that year at the age of sixty-two from working at General Motors for thirty years.

Later on, Harold met my husband. At first there was no problem between the two, until Harold asked if he could marry me. Brandon laughed that off, but then on my birthday Harold brought a brand new car to my home, a present. It was a red and white Pontiac. Harold knocked at the door, which Brandon opened. I could hear the conversation between the two.

"Hello, Mr. Matthews, is your wife home? I have a birthday present out in the front of the house. You come and see—it's a car."

I looked out the bedroom window and could see the beautiful car. Then I heard my husband say, "White man, Sylvia is my wife! Leave her alone before you force me to hurt you! Sylvia, come tell this old man something before I punch him out!"

Even after that, Harold still visited. He came with his daughter sometimes to go shopping and out to dinner, then riding around together until he moved out of town. Harold was my friend and needed my friendship, too. He spent a few dollars on me, but his daughter was pleased to see him so happy.

When I think of Bobby, I recall all the good songs we listened to as we drove around together to all the cities in the Westchester area of New York. Brandon went out with Bobby's sister and I went out with Bobby when I could find a way. The times I spent with Bobby were few and far between, sometimes even months apart. The first time I made up my mind to spend time with Bobby, I had walked into a nightclub, and there sat my husband with his lady friend. They were so occupied, I wasn't even noticed. I left, heading home, when

Bobby pulled up in his car and offered me a ride. We drove to a city just five miles away while he entertained me with his humor. We never set up dates, nor did he approach me secretly. Most of the times I saw Bobby, was either on my way to work, after work, or while waiting for a bus. There were times when I missed seeing him because Harold would drive up and take me home. They both watched after me and showed me great respect.

What I liked about each man was, I didn't have to find myself in a motel or somewhere out of the way. Our relationship was built on driving around, dining, or shopping for clothes. Bobby was soon trying to be more demanding of my time to the point I could not keep up with his itinerary. I was, after all, a married woman with children, and so we soon drifted apart. I had not seen Bobby for months and it nearly cost me my life. One night after working at the White Plains Hospital as a nurse's aide, I took the last bus to Tarrytown, but I got off in Ellsford hoping to see Bobby in the bar he often went to. He wasn't there so I ordered something to drink. The bartender said after the third drink, I could have the rest free of charge. I drank thirteen shots of 151 rum and soda. The hours passed and it was now closing time, but still no Bobby. Before I got off the bar stool, I noticed how tipsy I was. When I stepped down, it was like moon-walking, and I fell to the floor. A friend of Bobby's came over and helped me to stand on my feet.

"Let me take you home. Bobby is not coming in tonight, and you're drunk."

In the car, I passed out a few times—and upon getting out I dropped my paycheck in his car. Now at home, oh boy! I sure was drunk. I would have to get myself together before I could enter the back door, through which I could see my husband and his cousin playing cards in the kitchen. I shook myself and walked fast into the kitchen, passing them all. No one looked up, but we all spoke.

"Hi honey, who's winning? Got to go to the bathroom—see you in a minute."

The bathroom was to the right of Glenda's room where she was standing near her bedroom window.

I whispered to her. "Glenda, open up the window! I feel sick—hurry!"

The window went up and I vomited twice. On the third regurgitation, out the window I went, down two stories. My buttocks hit the concrete stairs, I bounced and slid in the vomit—when I got up, I smelled something awful.

Now I had to go back through the same door I had just come through—but this time I was noticed by everyone. Brandon got up and forcefully helped me to the bathroom, pushing me down into a tub of cold water. My head hit the faucet, knocking me out. That scar is yet on my head today.

It seemed our battles would never end. A few days later, Bobby's friend returned my paycheck, which I had dropped in his car. It made Brandon even more crazier. Not long after the man left, Brandon pinned my head between a wall and the bed. Out of anger, he bit me repeatedly all over my belly, leaving bite marks which became infected. I had to receive shots from my doctor to keep the poison from running through my body.

Dr. B. Dyeti asked me, "Why do you stay with that lunatic? Sylvia, you deserve better than what you get from that crazy man."

Like tit for tat, when Brandon could, he got back at me if I somehow got one over him. One evening I ran away, taking my children, and headed for Youngstown, Ohio. We got as far as the Harrisburg, Pennsylvania bus station. I called my mother and hoped she could wire enough money to get us the rest of the way home. While waiting, I met a man who stayed up with my boys while I slept off my exhaustion. The boys woke me up trying to get my attention.

"Mommy, see that man over there? He wants to buy us some food and I'm hungry. Please, Mom don't say no! Can we go with him?"

I looked over and saw this good-looking man looking back at me. "Tell him to come over so I can see just what he wants to do."

As I was talking to the boys, he headed toward our area.

"My name is Vegas and I make my living playing the horses. Today I will be going to Virginia to the race tracks. Would you like to come along, you and your boys? I can get a motel so you can rest while the boys and I go get some food. Lady, you can trust me."

With that I said, "Give me a minute with my boys."

We talked and they told me what Vegas had already done while I slept. When he came back over, I agreed to his plans and we headed toward the race track. Vegas fed us breakfast on the way and after getting a motel room, he and the boys went out for lunch. I slept and got myself a bath before they returned. Just before I could worry, I heard a knock at the door.

"How soon can you be ready? The races start in about twenty minutes!"

I opened the door and said, "Ready, let's go!"

Vegas smiled and off we went to the race track.

I had never heard about betting on horses at a race track, but that day would be my first and I enjoyed it. Vegas listened as I told him which horse would win. We won the Daily Double, which paid a great sum of money. Beginner's luck!

Because of the great sum of money we'd won, Vegas offered to keep me with him, but I decided to go back home. I thought I should call first to see what kind of mood my husband was in. I told him how we (myself and the boys) were held up in Harrisburg, Pennsylvania. He told me to come home because our income tax check had come in the mail, and he needed my signature. I promised Vegas I would return the next month, but it never happened—and I lost his phone number.

Money is a defense, but money can also be your enemy when it dictates your direction. I signed that check for my husband, but did not see a penny of it. Yet with him gone most of the time, I found peace of mind. Even with a change of attitude about how he would stop fighting me, he still took that money like all the other times and spent it foolishly.

Talking about peace, I learned to keep my distance from my husband. One morning I woke up early and instead of waking Brandon up so he could prepare to go to work, I waited, watching the time—so he would have only enough time to jump into his clothes and go off to his job. The General Motors plant was three blocks away from our home. As I watched the time, a strange thing happened. The curtains began to flutter from a soft breeze that came in the window. The air was so sweet and fresh, and the sun was just coming up in the east windows from the kitchen. All of a sudden, a transparent ball-like fire moved in motion toward me as I looked intently at it and lay in my bed very still.

"What is this?"

I heard a voice speak, and it seemed as if every word rippled.

"Sylvia, Sylvia, you're bad, do you hear me? You're bad! You had better be good!"

The ball of fire moved back, then moved up closer, again saying, "You're bad! You had better be good!"

My soul, that is, my inner mind, responded, *Yes, I hear you.*

It moved back and went out the same bedroom window, which was west of my kitchen, into the air. Up, up, and it vanished, like vapor. I wish more people could experience what I had seen that morning. Well...?

July 10, 1967 came fast, and I remember it so well. Brandon and I had returned home from the movies. With our babysitter gone, we got in bed to rest for the night. It was hot and with all the windows up, I could hear many noises coming from off the street. We lived near a much-traveled section of town across from the Tarrytown train station, near the General Motors plant entrance. It seemed I had fallen off to sleep as soon as my head hit the pillow. But then I remembered hearing someone.

"Get out, fire!"

But it was as if I were dreaming and slept all the harder until my husband yelled. "The house is on fire! I'll go get the boys—get up, get up!"

When I really woke up, fire was falling from the ceiling onto my bed. Now in a hurry, I stood on the floor as the flames lit up the bed. The bedroom and kitchen were engulfed quickly. I ran for the side hall door and opened it, but fire was dancing through the hall. I ran to the back kitchen door, where flames leaped off the upper porch onto the back entrance. I felt trapped until I turned to see part of my husband's leg go out the bedroom window. He had just put the boys out ahead of him. I ran, jumping over the fire, and swung my legs out the window, too. By now, the fire trucks had arrived and had their high-beam lights on the house and people stood in the street as tenants exited their apartments. The spotlights caught my naked behind as I came out with just a shirt on. One fireman put a blanket around me as we stood looking at the high flames engulfing our living quarters.

Our house was completely destroyed. We were completely distraught. What were we going to do now?

The Red Cross and friends each offered a place for shelter. Without much forethought, we chose to stay with friends, but after two nights we were asked to leave. They lived under a lease and it was not written into their contract to allow anyone outside their family to live with them. We turned to the Red Cross, but were turned down because we came to them two days too late. The next place we found to stay was deplorable. It was in the basement of our friend's parents' home. There we were climbing onto our bed in order to enter the small room, since only a bed and dresser could fit, leaving a narrow space to stand in. The bottom drawers could not be opened because there was not enough room to pull them out. The boys slept near the bottom of the bed, on a couch-chair. The room was kept warm by a small heater. We had to climb two flights of stairs to share the kitchen. The people upstairs would get into our food, the little we had, and sometimes we had to wait until they finished cooking before I could cook, so that we could eat. I hated every moment of living the way we did in that home. To make an already volatile situation worse, I was pregnant again, and now had to stop working for a while. The fire, climbing the stairs daily, and the pressure of having lost everything, including my husband, put me in such a bad state of mind, I could have snapped. I could not handle depression, but I learned how, and because I had so much of it, I made it a stairway to climb out.

We needed assistance from the Department of Human Services—I never even knew such a place existed. It was within walking distance and so up the hill I walked. Upon arriving there I filled out the necessary paperwork and applied for help—and it wasn't before long I was told there was nothing they could do for me. I was so angry, I told them I would bring my children and leave them there, then they would have to do something. With that, a case worker came out and told me she would come and look my situation over, and if I really needed help, I could get it. My emotions were on edge and after leaving, I cried all the way home. I knew the case worker would detest seeing my living conditions. She met me as planned and I took her as far as the door, but before I could open it, she shouted, "I've seen enough! Come back tomorrow!"

The next morning, I received an emergency check, which was used for an apartment in Ossinging. The Red Cross also gave me a clothing voucher with the stipulation that the only thing I could get was a bathing suit, and would have to go barefoot for the rest of the summer. I could not believe what I was hearing. So with the voucher, I purchased a dress and a pair of shoes. The children, too, received some clothing. Thank God for the check and voucher. But just the thought of going barefoot and wearing only a bathing suit threw my emotions way out in the lily white fields.

Chapter 7

Experience worketh patience, and that we needed. After getting the apartment we needed furniture so I went downtown to a furniture store and ordered a bedroom set. That evening, a repossessed set of bedroom furniture was delivered, which we were to have until the furniture I ordered, came in. It turned out to be a blessing because we didn't have to pay for the furniture we had not ordered.

With such a nice apartment now I tried to return to work. After a few weeks, I found myself in the emergency room threatening to miscarry my pregnancy. The doctor ordered me on bed rest and told my husband to refrain from sexual contact. That night Brandon was more sexually aggressive than usual. Early in the morning, I went to use the bathroom—and as I was cleaning myself, I felt the baby's leg hanging from my body. In the hospital the doctors tried to induce labor, but nothing happened. After hours had gone by, the intern came and told me they had to get the dead fetus out, because I would soon die from the poison if it ran through my body. Without giving me pain medication, the intern shoved his arm up into my belly and pulled the fetus out, detaching its body from its head. I had never heard of such things happening, much less to me, and to say this was a nightmare, is a huge understatement.

A few weeks later, at home recuperating, I could hear my older son Marvin calling, "Mom, come quickly! It's Lee, hurry Mom!"

At first it was like a dream, but his voice became clearer as I woke up, so I got out of bed and ran to where the children slept. There lay Lee with only the whites of his eyes showing. He was rigid and his tongue protruded from his mouth. Dried blood was on the base of his nose. My first reaction was to pick him up and shake him back to life.

"Oh, he's dead! Call the police!" I shook him more.

"Hurry! Come! My son! My son!"

The police were there in no time. I ran to the police car with my son wrapped in my arms. "Please hurry!" I cried as I shook him frantically.

The siren was on and we moved quickly to Phelps Memorial Hospital. The nurses in the emergency room quickly took Lee out of my arms and pushed me away from behind the curtains as they worked on my son. The only question in my mind was, "*How did this happen?*" My mind wandered to the evening before. Brandon had hit Lee in the face with one of his judo chops because he would not eat the garbage he fixed for them. The boys told me how cruel Brandon had been to Lee, how he slammed his head into the wall with the side of his large hand. Fortunately a team of doctors revived my son behind those curtains. After that event, I knew the authorities had been alerted and I knew we were being very closely scrutinized.

A sequence of torture and mishandling of the boys and myself went on. I was told much later on, how Brandon would squeeze the boys until they turned blue, then he threatened to kill them if they told anyone. Bruises and marks were found on their bodies and it seemed that during this period, I was constantly living in danger of having my boys taken away. We had been followed by day and watched at night by the detectives. While I was at work, a detective would come during lunch and check on how things were going in my home. Brandon was not aware we had protection so he continued his routine, handling us like dogs.

One night I stopped over in Nyack, New Jersey, across the bridge from Tarrytown to have a few moments to myself. I saw Bobby there with his lady friend. We spoke briefly, then he went back with whatever he was doing. I got up and headed home. When I pulled up in front of my apartment, Bobby and his girlfriend pulled up behind me. I got out and he did, too.

"Bobby, go home! You're going to get me in trouble with my husband. Just don't do this! What will it benefit you?"

Brandon opened the door. "Yo, man, what's going on? You with my wife?"

Bobby spoke up. "Yeah man, I followed her home to see that she got in safe. My lady is sitting out in the car waiting for me." They shook hands and Bobby left.

Brandon yanked at my clothes to pull me into the apartment. I wasn't even able to get a word out before he punched me. From twelve midnight until two in the morning, he beat and kicked me—even knocking a hole in the wall using my head! When the abuse was finished Brandon locked me in my bedroom where I lay unconscious for three days. A nurse who lived across the street came and confronted Brandon, after he answered the door.

"Get out of my way! I know your wife is in here. Let me take her to the hospital, dead or alive. Move so I can get to her!" This was told to me later when the nurse and her family invited me to their home for dinner.

At the hospital I regained consciousness long enough to sign papers for Brandon's arrest. For twenty-nine days I lay unconscious. It was said my brain was scrambled in my head and my clothes had been beaten into my flesh. My face was indistinguishable and the doctors thought I would never be normal again. The hospital administration wanted to institutionalize me for life, and if it hadn't been for Dr. Hill, I might still be there. My visits to Dr. Hill were a pleasure, for I was released from his care and he sent in his final report so I could get my boys back home with me.

My children were placed in a foster home until I was able to care for them again. My brother let his girlfriend, Smokey, a nurse, come home with me from the hospital because I could not be left alone for one minute.

One night, Smokey was paid by my next door neighbor, Mr. Copland, to leave the door open while she went to the store so he could come in and take advantage of me. From the night of the beating up until this time, I knew nothing nor anyone, but while this man was raping me, he held my body up in a position which caused the back of my neck to snap. Whatever he did, I snapped back to myself and scared him to death.

"Get off me now before I kill you...!" I won't repeat all I said, but he had to pay me for a while to keep my mouth shut.

Brandon remained in county jail until his hearing. The judge read all the counts against him and turned to me, asking what I felt about all this.

"We find your husband unstable and dangerous to society. He is a paranoid schizophrenic with multiple personality disorder."

I listened, but didn't understand a word. I knew he was all-out crazy; that went with the above. I lived with him night and day, but who could I turn to with him out of my life? I had been thrown out at such an early age and I never believed I could live alone, yet I realized I had been alone all this time. Maybe if I had one person to stand with me during the hearing, I could have accepted the judge's ruling. Instead I felt so sorry for all that had happened and asked for his release if he promised not to harm us again.

Chapter 8

Satan desires to sift you as wheat, and the wolves are out to devour any helpless weakling they can get. I felt I slept with the beast of a man.

Brandon was on his best behavior when he returned home from jail, but soon his promises of how he would treat us turned into lies. Maybe it was the girls he messed around with after he became a cab driver. Whatever it was, I no longer cared. I took the boys to Youngstown, never to return. I stayed with my parents for a few weeks. I had not been home for a long time and seeing a few of my friends was a delight.

Etta was one of the friends who had helped push me in the car that horrible night I was gang raped, but I forgave her. She came by one night to visit. I had heard she had been in jail and we talked about why. The conversation took a sudden twist when Etta made a pass at me. Needless to say, I was shocked, but didn't allow it. She was quite insistent and we began fighting right there in the living room. We ended up in the kitchen where my mother found us, with me holding a knife over her.

"Girl, put that knife down and Etta leave my home! Now!"

My mother had told me years ago there was something wrong with that girl, but she never made it plain.

I found a job as a barmaid on the west end of town. I received a twenty dollar bill as a tip from a man named Moody, which I'll later go into. It was while I worked at this place that I saw Jerome once again. He had recently been released from prison and we took up an interest in one another again. But when he started that old talk about hitting the streets for him, I changed direction and the last thing I told him was, "You need God in your life."

At the time, I had no idea it would be Jerome who would be the one to pray and bring me to the place where he and I could praise the Lord together as sister and brother.

But before I came from the *guttermost* to the uttermost, I still had to experience some more horrible things.

I got another job and was to start working that very next week as a nurse's aide at Southside Hospital. I was required to take a physical examination, which I did. The doctor was standing in front of me going over the results.

"You can start working this Monday, but you need prenatal care. Try the clinic here so we can watch you."

I was startled and left to go home to the apartment I had just rented. While waiting for the bus, standing in the rain, I made up my mind then that I wouldn't have this baby!

I was cold when I reached my upstairs apartment. I went to my closet, took a coat hanger and headed to my bathroom. I'll let you, dear reader, imagine what I next tried. My attempts to induce an abortion failed. The apartment was cold for the heat hadn't been turned on yet. Instead of going to my mother's, I laid on the springs of the bed frame, took my coat, and placed it over my body. It was damp and cold, but I slept there two nights, alone, not to be bothered. Monday morning soon came and crawling on the floor, I went down the steps to the back door where I heard voices.

"Help!" I cried as I opened the door.

That morning I was admitted to the same hospital at which I should have started working, with pneumonia.

Moody came to visit me.

"I found you! Why didn't you tell someone you were sick? It took calling around to find you." He handed me a bouquet of roses and a beautiful robe, both of which were very much needed.

"Listen, I have some furniture for your apartment and we've got plenty of places to go, so hurry and get well, okay, honey?" He leaned over to kiss me.

His visit gave me another rope to pull up and gain strength, and my pregnancy finally terminated.

Moody was a brick mason who made good money and spent it, too. We traveled to see his friends after work, ate out and at home in my apartment, and watched television. My mother lived a few blocks away and she looked after my children when I dated Moody. The one thing Moody told me was, "Never spend my money on cheap things—always buy the best. I work too hard to see my hard-earned money go to waste."

With all Moody did for me, there was one thing I could not tolerate—his Black Bull and how he hemmed me in. He was a good working man, but an alcoholic. He loved women, food, and alcohol.

One night after I returned from bingo and sent him home, I looked out my bedroom window, and there sat Moody in his car watching my house. We only dated, but he watched my every move, with him or without him. I told Moody I would not be a bird in a cage, not for all the money in China, nor could he govern me as if I were his wife.

That morning before he went to work, Moody came in and we talked about how he was sleeping in his car with one eye open, trying to catch my act. As he talked, the phone rang and Moody picked it up as if it belonged to him. On the other end was my father, and he joked with Moody. Before I could get him to understand it was my father, Moody left mad, but came back all out of sorts.

"Hey, watch your temper! You have no right!"

Before I knew it, I had hit him on his head with the receiver. "Get out of my apartment, now!"

The conversation turned into a heated argument. My father came in laughing and told Moody he was leaving while still holding his head in his hands. "Man, I was joking and you took it wrong. I always play on the phone like that with my children. Sorry you felt like that."

As he and Dad talked, I started calling people to come get what furniture they wanted. I also called Brandon back in New York.

"Come on back home, you and the boys." Brandon was anxious to see us again. In a few hours that apartment was empty and that evening we were headed to Ossinging.

From one pit to another. I often wondered why I chose to return and sleep with a beastly man. The things Brandon did were horrible. Maybe I thought we were to stay together until death did us part. I learned to maneuver around my husband, to find a sound mind to live normally, and so I let him run free with no questions asked.

Work in Westchester County, New York, was easy to find. I did a lot of domestic jobs. Some jobs were beneficial. The Hillelsons, the Steinfields, and the Reader's Digest Corporation, all in Pleasantville, New York, at one time or another hired me, along with three hospitals.

I cared for Mrs. Hillelson's mother who taught me how to make clear chicken soup using the white of an egg. I then cleaned and helped during their Jewish holidays. It was a privilege to serve them because they treated me more like a daughter. Mr. Hillelson would do extra things for me in exchange for a back rub. However he would not go beyond a good back rub since his faith in God and their beliefs did not permit him to behave contrary to the Jewish Law. The best turkey I ever ate was the turkey which had been cooked in an outdoor fireplace by Mr. Hillelson. I received many clothes from that family, including a wedding dress. They tried hard to adopt me into the Jewish faith, and I would have inherited from their estate had I done so. Their love for me was so genuine.

The Steinfields were introduced to me by the Hillelsons. I worked for them mostly on Fridays, starting early in the morning, and cleaning the house from top to bottom, not leaving a stone unturned. Sometimes there would be a rest break if time allowed, then we would begin setting up tables for supper. This was routine, and each month on a Friday, we would feed the Jewish children from different homes in the area who attended the Pleasantville Cottage School. The Steinfields were also good people. They were real enough to never talk about that black and white issue, because it only painted things gray and gray is so depressing. I learned there are no inferior or superior classes of people. For a while I felt perplexed to be around them, but they showed true love. I learned to see cotton is cotton as chicken is chicken, and the only difference is its grade or quality. We all own nothing, but the plot of ground from which we are made and to which we shall return because we belong to He who is Supreme, He who is creator of all things—God, whose name is Emmanuel. God is with us; He is Jesus, His earthly name given to mankind.

Thank God for caring people, for with each bout I had with my husband or sickness, I found Mr. and Mrs. Hillelson there for me. Sometimes I was too ashamed to let them know all I had to endure. They taught me how to trust and be trusted, and even after I moved back to Youngstown, we kept in touch. In my confession, they did all they could to keep me from going down. One of the Hillelson family gave me a trunk with different items in it. One of the items was a box of tarnished old forks, knives, and spoons dating back to the1800s. I valued that gift and said I would not give any of the items away. Unfortunately, I did, and found out later that the collection was worth thousands—a costly mistake.

Chapter 9

While at work I found great relief, but at home, trouble stood at my door. The boys and I were happiest when Brandon stayed away for long hours. It got to the point where an elderly lady sat under my window and prayed for the family. It was her daughter who took the time to tell me if she ever caught me doing drugs, she would hurt me real bad. I had to live on a mental high, and kept my thoughts elevated by saying things were going to get better; that drugs, alcohol, or anything like it, would only dampen my alarm system. I had to be alert at all times because I realized drugs and alcohol could knock at my door at any given time, living with Brandon.

One morning the praying woman's daughter called me to her apartment and told me to watch her. She took a bottle cap, placed a baking soda-looking substance into this cap, and with a lighter she placed fire under the cap, turning the solution red. She then took a needle and after drawing the solution out with a needle, she made her veins pop up and shot that red solution up into her veins. Heroin—the devil's juice. Josephine was her name, but we called her Jo. This nice girl turned crazy the moment she shot the juice up her vein.

"You—!" She called me a dirty word. "If I wanted, I could have your no-good husband. When are you going to wake up to reality? This freak of a man is messing all over you. Girl, if I ever caught you doing drugs, I would kill you myself."

Sweat was dripping off her face as she yelled at me.

"I hate what I do, but this is my life. I'm on my way to the Big Apple and I got to be out of my mind to face the things I do. But you!"

She was now in my face.

"You stay clean! Don't let your husband or any other man give you this junk. Oh yeah, it's the devil's juice. You can't stand me, huh? Can you? I hate myself too, but…"

She called me names that aren't worth repeating. Then she pushed me onto the davenport and sat on me. With glassy eyes, she carried on something awful.

"Call your husband, that dog, down here, let me show you what he's like! Wipe those tears, and shut up!" She reached for a few tissues. "Stop that crying and get out of here. Now look, don't even touch this paraphernalia. You got so much going for you, just leave!"

Her voice rang in my heart for a long time. The last I heard, her boyfriend OD'd. Her mother soon moved and another couple moved into that apartment, who also became close to me.

I knew my husband wasn't any good, but that didn't take away the fact he was my husband. I felt something was wrong, but couldn't always put my hands on it. My so-called neighbor friends knew more, but wouldn't utter a word to me. There was one young lad who came to play with the boys, and while in the bedroom one afternoon, I overheard him.

"Your daddy is my daddy, too. He climbs into my mother's bedroom all the time and they sleep together."

I stood still at the kitchen sink as he told the boys what he knew about his mother and my husband. With that information, I kept my distance from my husband. It was strange when a few days later Brandon came into the kitchen and asked me to take Geraldine to the hospital because she had burned herself badly. Geraldine was the young lad's mother, the woman my husband was spending a lot of time with. I knew in my heart he had done something to her.

"Brandon, she is your woman! Whatever went on between the two of you, you handle it. Go climb in her window and take her to the hospital yourself. You burned her, you take her!"

I couldn't believe I spoke so strongly. He stood threatening me for that raggedy woman and for the first time, I withstood his threats. I told him what I knew and told him to get out of my face. He was shocked and began to make amends for his behavior. From that time on, I withdrew from having anything to do with my husband as his wife.

August 10th was another day of mishaps. The boys were playing with matches under a bed and caught the neighbor's apartment on fire. We had to vacate our apartment for a while. It wasn't too long because it was only smoke-damaged. We stayed with my neighbors who had moved into Josephine's old apartment. Nancy was very nice, and she and I got along well. Her parents were wealthy and she was interesting to me because that summer, she wore only one dress and a skimpy pair of shoes all summer long. When her inheritance came, she bought clothes and a General Motors car, then she and her husband Robert moved to Texas.

After the fire in August, we moved back into our apartment. Marvin came home from school one day with bloodshot eyes. He had fallen out of a tree while playing. His playmate told me he fell and landed on his head with his legs and feet sticking straight up in the air. Marvin was admitted into the hospital with a severe brain concussion. This was one time Brandon was not the cause of the injury.

Still, it had gotten bad living with this man. I tried to leave more than once, too, but found myself right back with him. One night I put urine in a bucket and mixed with it lye, then waited for my husband to come home, get in bed, and fall asleep. He did just as I wanted and fell asleep without any clothing on. I took the bucket in my hands and started toward the bedroom. I could see him clearly as I stepped toward the room. All of a sudden, a glass wall came from out of nowhere. *Where did this come from, where?* I felt the pot hit the glass and heard it ring.

A voice said, "Vengeance is mine! I will repay! Don't put that blood on your hands!"

When I put the solution down, my hands turned bright, like fire. I stood looking at my hands; they were aglow, bright red. As I looked, the voice spoke again with authority.

"Don't put the blood on your hands!"

In that split second, I knew my hands were going to be used for something special one day. Then a calm came over me and I settled down in the bed beside my husband as if nothing had happened. I was sick of my husband by now and longed for this marriage to be over.

Nine months had passed since the judge had warned Brandon that he was not to harm or lay a hand on either the children or myself and if he did, he would have to leave the premises.

One day I returned home from work, prepared supper, and called the boys in to eat. They had always tried to be obedient and were really the best boys a mother could have.

"Sit down!"

I grabbed Marvin by the hand to put some force behind my command.

"Why are you resisting me?" I asked.

"We can't, Mom. Dad beat us today with a broom handle across our buttocks." The word "beat" rang out loud.

"What do you mean, beat you? For what? Let me see!"

I saw and I screamed, "Oh my God, why did he do this? Didn't I tell you to stay out of his way!"

I grabbed them all together and held them close as I cried.

"Why would he do this to you? Tomorrow we will go to the judge." Brandon had beat the boys by laying them over his lap and hitting them repeatedly, hundreds of times, causing blisters twice the size of their butts to form. The next morning I took the boys to see the judge. He gave me a court order, placed in a manila envelope.

"Sylvia, you give this to your husband when he comes home. Don't open it, just place it where he can see it, okay? Do as I say!"

That night I laid the envelope on the table, hoping he would come home. He hadn't been there since the beating. It was the coldest night in November, 1968, when he finally came home, acting as if nothing had happened. I, too, acted as if nothing had been done.

"What's for supper, girl? Fix me a plate. Hey, what's this?" he asked as he sat down at his usual place.

"Open it up and see."

By now he had read the contents.

"What does this mean—I have to leave?"

I was no longer scared of what might go down.

"Yes!" I said. "Leave and do that tonight—like right now. Leave! I don't need your kind around me anymore—just go!"

I watched him pack and for a moment, came close to saying, "*No, don't go*," but I weighed the years in that second and didn't say a word. The door shut behind Brandon as he left for good. The door not only shut, but ended ten years of hell.

Chapter 10

Looking over my married life with Brandon, I wondered how I made it through so many problems and difficult situations. I also see there was no love, just tolerance, one for the other. Loneliness was part of my life, and even as I write, I find myself lonely. Maybe God intended I live times like this so He could get more of my attention for Himself. I learned to communicate with Him from being sick and seeking help on my knees so many times. It wasn't the *"knee-ology"* but the results that taught me how to endure the pain and agony. Besides the things I had endured with my husband, I also had been hospitalized so much for too many illness. It seems as if I have experienced just about every illness there is.

I suffered from heart ailments. The one heart failure I recall occurred while I was living in Ossinging. I had been admitted into the hospital and progressively grew worse. It had gotten so bad, in fact, that my parents were notified I only had a short time to live. My parents sent for my brother who lived in New York City. Before he walked into my room I went through a most challenging experience.

My kidneys had stopped functioning, which led to heart failure. For three days they had not functioned and my heart grew weak; death was moments away. Dr. Dyeti came, making his daily visit.

"Sylvia, how do you feel today?" he asked, looking at me through the oxygen tent.

"I feel better than I ever felt in my life. Can't you see me up in this cloud?" Yes, I was up in a cloud looking at myself laying in an oxygen tent and talking to Dr. Dyeti.

"What cloud?" he asked. He called for a nurse to order an EKG. Watching the reading with only weaving lines, no rhythmic beats, a blood transfusion was ordered. Blood transfusions had been given several times during many of my illness, so this was not uncommon for me. The urinal bag was flat and I lay breathless, until an *unusual man* moved into my room. He was not a man such as we see each day. He moved with grace. He didn't seem to be in a hurry, and his movements were soft and swift. I watched him move toward my bed as I looked through the plastic that made up the oxygen tent. He was not a doctor, nor a visitor from some other room, nor a priest. He wore a long dark robe and spoke as he touched my foot: "Live on!"

I know what I saw, but I fear to say he was God!

The voice I've heard many times before. I saw Him as a ball of fire, felt Him in the cloud, and then saw him as a priestly looking man. This would not be my last encounter with Him: now He had come to touch me, extending my life.

Darkness is so obscuring in most lives that we can't see Him. Yet He is so near, we cannot comprehend. The word of God says it like this: "Oh, the depth of the riches both of the wisdom and knowledge of God! How unsearchable are his judgements, and his ways past finding out." (Rom. 11:33)

Who is this, who would visit me at my lowest ebb and speak life into my weak and failing body? At home my recovery took weeks to months. I had to crawl around, pulling up just to use the bathroom. The boys maintained the best they could. Help never came. It took almost seven months for me just to walk, but after I could make it to a store, which was a block away. I eventually recovered again…

Chapter 11

Anna, Lucile's sister, called me on the phone to ask me out with the girls from the neighborhood.

"Girl, Brandon is gone and now you can step out for a little fun."

I told her no at first, then thought about it. I called her back.

"What time will you be leaving? Send your sister Lucile over to baby-sit when you're ready to go, then stop here for me."

Living a single life would not put me into the category with some others—you know, single, disengaged, and wild. My children dampened that atmosphere. Having a good time was not my appetite, nor did I want to be pawed on by every man who crossed my path. I wasn't the worst looking girl, but found out good looks can draw honey and honey attracts super flies which go about bloating sweet meat.

We met outside my apartment and walked to the dance hall about four blocks away. I took a seat and ordered a drink. The music was loud, and the people were out to have fun. A hand reached over my shoulder toward Anna, then I heard a man's voice ask, "Would you like to dance?"

I watched each time she got up to enjoy herself. As soon as she sat down, she was back up again. Yes, I did feel I wasn't getting any attention, so I changed my drink to something stronger. Still Anna received more hands to dance than me. She was fair, with a soft beige complexion, light blue eyes, and a tall stature. I was short, with a pecan tan complexion, brown eyes and nappy hair, but we both had the same needs and desires. Finally, a hand reached over to me.

"Sorry, sir, I think I'll just sit this one out," I said, full of pride.

It was a fast dance and I couldn't do some of those new steps. As I looked on, I noticed one man whom I had turned down watching me from a distance. Soon he sent me a drink, which I refused.

"Tell him I've had enough, but will try a slow dance instead."

He came right over and I explained I had not danced for some time, nor did I want to embarrass him on the floor.

"All you have to do is follow me and enjoy yourself. I've got it covered."

When I sat down, Anna and the other girls laughed at the expression on my face.

"You really looked good on that floor with ah...oh, what is his name? Y'all dance like you belong to each other, but did you get his name, girl?" Anna jumped up and rushed over toward him, but stopped midway. She had another dance, so I got up and went over to where he stood, then pulled at his coat. He was talking to another girl.

"Excuse me, but what is your name? The girls I sit with want to know." He turned, looking at me with delight.

"My name is Little C. It stands for Cohen."

I later learned his first name was Henry. He had a light Southern accent, and because of all the noise, I could hardly hear all of his conversation. He was tall, dark brown, and thin. He looked sharp with black slacks and a long black leather coat with fur on the collar. I heard him say, "I'm a black Jew."

"So what has that to do with you being a person?" I hit a note for more conversation.

It was closing time and I pushed ahead of my friends because crowds have always been a problem with me since I lose my balance, so I try to be the first out. I stood on the walkway waiting for the girls to exit. Cohen caught up with me.

"Would you like to go for breakfast up in Peekskill?" The girl who had been standing with him when I pulled his coat, was there beside him and heard him ask me to go for breakfast.

"Don't let Pearl be a bother to you—she won't do a thing, and I'll see that you get home. We're going to an after-hour joint where we can eat some good Southern food. My mother is the cook."

I turned to look for the girls, but they were too busy getting together with fellows they'd met. Anna did walk over and suggested I go ahead with Cohen.

"We'll see you up there!"

I hesitated for a moment, but Lucile was with the boys—I knew they were in good care so I opted to go.

"See, lady, I told you to come on."

The car door opened and Cohen helped me into the front seat, although I sort of resisted him because of his girlfriend, who stayed so close to his every move.

"Pearl is just a friend—she won't mind, huh, Pearl?"

The girl nodded her head and climbed into the backseat.

"Women, move it over so I can ride, too!"

Cohen was so busy getting us girls seating, he hadn't gotten in the car yet.

When we arrived, Little C. and I remained in the car. It was late and I told him I had to go home to my children. He said he would get the driver and some food, then take me home.

"At least come in long enough to meet my mother and get some of her Southern fried chicken."

With one arm extended and his other hand on his hip, he said, "Grab a wing." I was a little frightened because I felt trapped with a man I knew very little about. He felt me resist him and stopped, then as I stood up on my feet, getting out of the car, he grabbed me up into his arms.

"You didn't mean that?" He stole a kiss and then turned me loose. "You're afraid of me? That's all right—you have the right to be."

He paid the charge to get in the place, then after meeting his mother we found the driver, just like he said.

As we were leaving, he told Pearl, "I'll see you later, after I get back."

I learned a lot about him as we drove back. He was from Georgia and worked for General Motors, but couldn't read a lick. At my apartment he gave me a telephone number at which I could reach him if I changed my mind, for I had said no to his sexual advances.

One day I stopped by his home to say hello, but he wasn't there. So I put him plum out of my mind until the boys came home a few days later with new tennis shoes on their feet.

"Hey, where did you get those shoes?"

They were joyous. "That man down the street named Cohen. He took us shopping with him when we saw him downtown."

One of Cohen's friends who knew Brandon told him about my boys. Cohen saw the need and bought them shoes. I picked up the phone and dialed his number. I wanted to personally thank him. Cohen answered and as I started speaking, the line on the other end clicked off. *That's odd, why would he hang up on me?* But no sooner

could I think those words when I heard a knock at the front door. I heard the boys let someone in.

"Who is that?" I yelled.

It was Little C. Before I had a chance to say anything, he immediately started talking.

"Whatever it takes, I'll prove to you how I feel. Yes, I got those shoes and will do more if you let me. I can help out around the apartment, and I could get your car in the backyard started, if you fix a lunch daily for me. Your apartment—I can paint it, too. Just have my lunch ready by three o'clock, okay?"

That weekend I went to New York to pick up material to make earrings, which I had been creating and selling on my job while employed at the Reader's Digest Corporation. Cohen offered to watch the children until I got back. In the city I met I-Da, a Jamaican. I knew him for a short time before my husband and I broke up. He and a group of men sold earrings too, and I could buy my material from them. However, I'd had a bad experience while on this particular trip to purchase merchandise.

I'd gone to their business and they sent me to buy some East Indian food, which was so good. I walked into that restaurant and purchased our favorite plates. After paying for the food I stepped back and then suddenly passed out. The next thing I knew, I had been pulled out of the restaurant and left on the sidewalk. My food was put in the car, and I asked them to please call the number I held in my hand.

"Tell them to come get me out of here."

I could not stand on my feet. I-Da soon came and drove me to Harlem Hospital. It was a mess. They examined me first for drugs, then to make sure I wasn't mentally ill. When they asked if I had done drugs, I-Da disappeared. Soon I was able to be released, the diagnosis being a kidney ailment. I was certain it wasn't drugs because I had poured out a soda that had been laced with a white substance. I had seen it when one of the Jamaicans dumped it into my drink. I had just taken a look over my shoulder, and saw him put the "white girl," as the drug was called, in my drink. I let that drink sit on the counter.

After recovery, I went back to the city once again, but this time I-Da asked me to go on a run with him. Not knowing about the state of

New York, I found myself up in the hills outside the city of Albany. I believe to this day that ride was meant to be the day of my death. But as we sat in the car and talked, I-Da had a change of mind. Maybe he thought I knew too much, so he would have to kill me, but I was ignorant as to what he talked about. I knew about over-the-counter drugs, but I knew nothing about street drugs and still haven't learned enough. Having convinced him of my innocence, we drove back to my apartment.

As we walked into the apartment, Cohen was on the couch, asleep. I told I-Da he was there to watch my boys and fix up my apartment. Cohen got up and met I-Da, then he called me into the kitchen.

"Sylvia, get rid of that man now or I will."

So I ordered them both out, then turned in for the night myself. The next morning, I could hear the boys in the kitchen with Cohen fixing breakfast. The boys had let him back in.

Christmas was coming up the next week, and we sat to discuss what we planned to do. Cohen didn't say much about the holidays, but he did more than any person could do, seeing as how he just met us in the first week of December. I had planned to make it as just another day. I hated the holidays because there never served in the homes as to what they stood for. I could give, but... If I visited a home, I ended up cleaning up. If I visited, I could always count on my hands. We got the car running and I helped Cohen study so he could get his driver's license. Cohen called me to talk about getting a tree and all the trimmings and how we could spend the coming New Year down in the Big Apple. He would pay the babysitter and take me shopping that weekend in the city to shop for a new dress, one I could wear out that New Year's Eve.

Cohen was so kind in helping to see that my children and I had a good Christmas. The tree and trimmings he bought, then he helped put it up. He also, after learning I had things in layaway, paid to get them out for me. With all he did, I went out for him, big time. His kindness warmed my heart. For once I felt being around a man, I was secure.

We went shopping in the Big Apple as planned and I found a most beautiful blue dress for the New Year. After that, we started seeing more of each other. I fixed him lunch and at night he came to have his reading lesson checked.

1969 was a mixed-up year and once again I found myself pregnant in the spring of 1970. Because of my condition, Cohen and I decided to move into the apartment above his mother's and across the hall from Pearl. This pregnancy, not unlike the others, kept me in and out of the Grassland Hospital every other week or so. Cohen was a big help caring after the boys during my absences. His mother and family helped, too.

With Pearl living right across the hall in another apartment, I managed to ignore the loud outbursts she made every now and then. Cohen would talk to her about leaving me and the boys alone. It became uncomfortable and rather nerve-wracking, but we stuck it out until my birthday. I had taken a bus to do some shopping in White Plains, New York. After taking the last bus home, Cohen's mother beckoned me to come into her apartment for a minute. I thought she had the boys, so I went in.

"Surprise!" A crowd of people rushed toward me.

I covered my mouth, which had dropped open. It was a surprise birthday party Cohen and his family gave me. The music started and I saw people who I'd least expect to come see me, dancing and having a good time. Money was pinned to my clothes and gifts were given; it was very nice. I was having so much fun, I'd neglected my boys and wanted to make sure they were doing okay. I stepped out the door to find Cohen and Pearl standing in the dark hall.

"What's this?" I said.

Cohen tried to explain, but I refused to listen. His sister took me back into the kitchen to calm me down.

"It ain't worth the trouble. Come on, let's just party!"

Seeing all the good food, I got myself together until the guests began to clear out, then I left, too.

The next morning, looking through the want ads, I found an apartment on Wardle Avenue in Yonkers, New York. By the following week, I had moved. Cohen tried to get me to understand there was nothing between he and Pearl as he helped me with the furniture. After getting me settled in my new place, he fell asleep on the couch. I didn't care; our relationship was torn apart. Pregnant and half-sick, I didn't care as long as he kept his distance. Carrying his baby meant nothing to me.

We had taken the third floor apartment and the landlady lived on the first floor with her daughter. She didn't mind me having a common-law marriage or anything else I might be involved in, because she, too, had a situation with her daughter, Rudine.

One day I went to pay my rent, and when I knocked at their door, I heard voices say, "Come in." As I stood waiting, someone opened the door and I walked in, then saw Rudine and her friends twisted together in bed, doing some strange things, with little shame.

"Have a seat. Mom is coming to get the rent, but meanwhile you can get a good look at what we like to do here."

They kept on as if I weren't there. Soon Rudine's mother came to me and took her rent money.

"Mrs. Cohen, don't be alarmed by what you see. My daughter is already pregnant and she and her husband like their friends to join them making love. Sometimes I get involved, too."

This girl was eight months pregnant! I couldn't believe the way she acted. I left, praying to never see that again. One day Rudine's husband climbed outside to the third floor, walking around looking in the windows, trying to see me. I ducked, keeping myself from his view, as he walked around looking into each room. I became afraid to live there and started hunting for another apartment, especially after the night I heard a car's motor quickly turning over and over. When I looked out the window, I could hardly see, but I heard them pushing a man's head into the racing motor. The man's screams were cut short, then I could barely make out what they were doing. They dragged that man into their basement and later placed him out on the street a few doors away.

It had been so hard to tell Cohen what was going on in that building. He would come home, then go right out. Nor could I get him to take time to talk with me about anything. The neighbors gave my son Marvin a Siamese chocolate point cat, and Cohen hated that blue-eyed cat.

"Sylvia, until you get that cat out of here, don't try to talk to me."

All I wanted was to tell him how bad the place was for my children. I wanted him to listen.

"Cohen, those people kill."

I could never get him or anyone else to listen to me when I needed them to hear. "Just listen!" But he would walk out.

I took a bottle of pills, muscle relaxers, which were supposed to help me rest for a few hours. They were so strong, that just one made me sleep for two days. I was so depressed, I took them all. My son found me on the top landing, dazed. With help, I was rushed to the hospital where I was pronounced dead on arrival. DOA. I had no heartbeat, no pulse, no reflexes. The doctor later told me later how my teary-eyed son pulled on his coat.

"Don't let my mommy die! She's all we got—do something, please!"

"Mrs. Matthews, if your son had not pulled at me like he did, you would not be alive today. We took a chance and pumped your stomach."

I looked at that doctor with thanks in my heart, but what kept going through my mind was how I fell into outer darkness, tumbling over and over with nothing to grab onto. I had left my body and was headed to another place—HELL! I saw the flames way down below just waiting for my entrance. My body, like everyone else's, has a soul which belongs to God. I heard my soul speak out for me.

"Don't let me die like this! I'll be good!"

When I came back to Earth, I woke up to a nurse slapping my face and saying, "You stay awake and drink this coffee!"

"Hey, I heard you the first time, woman. Don't hit me again!"

Later on, the doctor came in and sat beside me. "Young lady, did you try to kill yourself and leave those boys behind?" I heard him tell me what prompted him to pump my stomach.

"Doctor, I was upset with my common-law husband, but I'll be all right now."

He sat there looking at my file in his hands. "You can go home, but only because you didn't fight the nurse when you were coming out. We have put many people away for a long time after attempts like these. How soon can you get out of here?"

I got up, got dressed, called Cohen, signed out, and went home.

I was four months pregnant now and home with the same problems, but more tolerant. Mrs. Pue lived on the second floor, and each time I came in or went out, I had to pass her apartment. She often asked me for the shoe box of old tarnished silverware which sat on the top landing outside my apartment door. She worried me, so I simply said, "Go ahead, take those ugly things."

One day while on my way out, I noticed boxes piled up in her apartment.

"Mrs. Pue, why all these boxes? What're you doing, packing to move out, huh?"

We talked for a while, then she told me some shocking news.

"That shoe box blessed my husband and I—one knife was worth thousands, so we got enough to buy a house on the hill. As for you, Sylvia, get out too, girl."

Needless to say, I was devastated, but just another bad luck story for the sad life I was leading. I let it go with all the other baggage I had left behind in my life.

With all that went on in that apartment house, I did need to move and found another apartment at 250 Broadway in Yonkers. Just before I moved, another incident occurred. It had been said by the doctors I should abort my pregnancy because of tumors in my womb. This pregnancy was life-threatening for me.

It was now late August. Cohen came home from work earlier to dress and go out as usual. It was the beginning of the weekend and I remember watching him leave from my bedroom window as he reached his brand new car. Before getting inside, he turned and waved to me from the street. I suddenly felt a need to hurry to the bathroom and felt my water bag gush from me. *"Oh gosh, Cohen just left. I had better call a cab and get to Grasslands Hospital before something else happens."*

My neighbor said they would watch the boys until Cohen got home. I had no idea how much pain and complications would soon follow. At the hospital I was admitted and taken to the labor room.

It was late Friday when the doctor ordered me to be watched very closely.

"If her temperature goes over 101, call me right away," the doctor told the nurses.

An I.V. was started to induce labor, but that didn't happen. Soon, hours had passed. My temperature elevated and the doctor was called. I can't recall how long it took before my husband was told to come because complications had set in and I would need a Caesarian to have the baby. It was now Sunday and a decision would have to be made soon.

"Mr. Cohen, your wife may lose her life along with the baby. Her temperature is now 105, her kidneys have malfunctioned, and her heart is very weak. She has not dilated since early Saturday morning. She only has a few hours to live. You may go in to see her, and take the boys along with you."

My husband and the boys came in to say their good-byes. I felt no guilt for what had gone on, but here I was, at death's door. Again. The monitor attached to my stomach was disconnected because the baby's heart stopped beating. Then the doctor ordered all tubing disconnected, too.

"Sylvia, I don't know what your faith is, but you don't have long to be here. There is little more I can do. I can't even take the baby. You know it has died. Is there anything you want to say?"

I just stared at him helplessly. I had just told my family it was going to be all right. Was there a God somewhere? What else could anyone do? My life was doomed. It seemed I was going backward and had been cheated out of a good life. My heart was weak and my time was running out. After Cohen and the boys left the delivery room, I fell asleep. When I woke up, I could see the doctor in the corner of the room, writing at the counter.

"Kick! Put your feet on the side rails and grab the bars—push, push a little harder!"

Something in my head was instructing me. I pushed until I felt my heart about to burst. On the third try, the baby popped out.

A nurse walked by. "Doctor!" she yelled.

He looked up and came quickly over. The first thing he did was reach inside to pull out the placenta. It was all done with life-saving skill.

How could I be so irresponsible to let this happen?

Back on the ward with the other mothers made it even harder, but I was sure enough a sick girl. It took some doing to help me recover from that ordeal. My baby was buried before I came home. My mother helped Cohen lay Marrietta to rest.

We soon moved up on the hill in Yonkers, New York. Things went on as usual. Cohen ran the streets just as hard, to the point that I tolerated him as long as he paid the bills and kept his hands off me.

One day he did a floor show on me in front of his friends by slapping me down and stepping over me to go out that night. The very moment I got up off the floor, I reached for the phone and called my father to come get me out of Yonkers. "Enough is enough!"

For the first time my dad did something for me. He drove a U-Haul truck up from Ohio and loaded it with my belongings. When Cohen finally returned home early that morning, we were putting the last item in the truck. Cohen came over and took me by the arm, but I pulled away.

"Woman, what are you doing? Why are you doing this? Haven't I been good to you?"

"You fool," I said turning to him, "I'm sick of what you have been doing. Your interest is in the street, not here with me."

It was a combination of reasons and I finally had enough of his staying out until all hours and for days, not paying his part of the bills, and he was also an alcoholic. So long and good-bye. It should have been my final farewell, but I don't believe in burning bridges behind you. You never know—you may have to cross over them again.

Chapter 12

Youngstown, Ohio will always be home. Mom and Dad accommodated me the best they could. My monthly assistance checks were sent for four months, then I found a job working for the Elk's Club on the north side serving alcohol and beer to club members. The job paid well and the tips were good, and I could go to school in the mornings to better myself.

Cohen soon followed and tried to live in Youngstown, but he soon drove my black and white Thunderbird back to New York where he and his friends were found guilty of robbing a Howard Johnson's restaurant. My car was impounded and he got a fifteen-month jail sentence for that crime.

During the months Cohen was out of my life, I worked hard and attended college on Market Street. I achieved my G.E.D. and received certification for PBX switchboard or telephone operator, but I could never land a job in those fields. I learned to survive all my disappointments and when I failed in one area, I would accomplish in another. I learned how to get what was needed without borrowing or stealing, and I worked for what I desired. My family contributed what they could, but they, too, had to make ends meet. Maybe I did them a favor getting out of their hair at the age of fifteen or sixteen, but at least I could always get a meal from them. By now I felt better living on my own, so I got an apartment on West Warren Avenue.

At the Elks Club, Shirley, a co-worker, the captain of the Elks, and I, took a trip and checked into a motel in Toledo, Ohio. The captain and his staff were in one room, while Shirley and I had an adjacent room. After a meeting, we went to visit a bowling alley, where Shirley met a man. During their conversation, she informed the man where we were staying for the night. This trip would turn into another near disaster.

Both she and I had fallen asleep and I thought I was dreaming of a man feeling my legs. To my surprise, I reached at and grabbed a hand, pushing it off my thigh. Realizing it wasn't a dream, I got out of bed, headed to use the bathroom. While I sat on the commode, rubbing my eyes, I noticed the door was hanging from its hinges. Finished with my business, I moved slowly out of the bathroom. I was shocked to see my friend being raped. My thoughts ran wild as I looked at a gun laying on the floor halfway under the man's dress pants. The man was hurting her badly and had his hands cupped over her mouth so she could not scream out, but she muttered pained sounds.

He saw me look at his gun, then jumped off of Shirley long enough to grab it. "Both you and she could die if you say a word! Don't move at all—just watch."

He was still holding on to Shirley to remount her. When he finished, he dressed and took her hostage, warning that if I did anything foolish, she would die. It was some time later when Shirley finally returned. She was shaken pretty badly.

"Call the captain, Syl!"

The captain came and we blurted out all that had happened. Shirley spoke with guilt and said she'd made a mistake.

"I trusted this man because he told me his line of work—a detective, hogwash!" Shirley laid across her bloodstained bed and cried.

Returning to Youngstown, I pledged I would not trust another man ever again in my life. I would handle things for myself. I stuck to that until Ricky, a boy who played with me in the backyard on Cleveland Street, crossed my path again. I had not seen him since he'd shot his father at the age of fourteen and had returned from living in California since the shooting. He was a truck driver and lived close to my apartment off Warren Avenue, on Hillman Street. It was good to see an old playmate who was trying to make ends meet, too. We found ourselves talking on my porch regularly. Often late hours at night, after I got off from work, he would come for a few drinks or wait for me and follow me home. If I ever loved a man in my life, it would be Ricky, but he always came in and out of my life. Of course this period of time I spent with Ricky was joyous. We never planned to live common-law, it was just convenient for him to stay over while I attended school on Market Street. Ricky started by sleeping on the couch and then came to a time we found ourselves living together.

The day Ricky left my home was when his brother told me he was stealing my tips to purchase his girlfriend an engagement ring. When I talked it over with him, I told him to take his belongings and leave and not ever return until he knew what he wanted in life. Ricky got a house on the east side of town, and one night he called me to come over to talk with him.

"Sylvia, I love you, but I need you to understand me. I need you to wait. I don't want to hurt you, nor my girl. She's a Christian and her parents would kill me if I disappoint them.

"I will break this engagement off if I know you..."

Shh," he whispered, "don't say a word, please. It's my lady." Ricky got out of bed and stood at the top of the stairs.

"Hi, honey. Why didn't you call before you came over? I'm taking a shower. Go get us a pizza and we can spend the evening together, okay, honey? The money is in the dish on the table, right there. See it, see you in a few."

On his way back, he copped a plea.

"Look, Ricky, I can't wait under these conditions. Don't ever call again, unless you end your relations with this and any other woman you might have." Time lapsed before I would see Ricky again.

Ricky married that girl and they stayed together five months, so I heard. The last time I laid my eyes on Ricky was the day I entered the side door of Pentecostal Church on Oakhill Avenue. I heard a voice from the distance and recognizing it, I turned. "Ricky!"

"Hi Babe!"

He was sitting in his car curbside. I opened the church door inviting him to come inside with me. "This is the best place we can go together to get our lives straightened out!"

As he sat looking out the car window, he spoke, "Hey girl, I'll catch you on the rebound—ain't ready yet. Think I'll head out of town. Bye."

For a moment we both paused as if to join each other, but those few moments made the difference for the next seventeen years.

Maybe I never knew what true love was—until I met Jesus.

Chapter 13

"For the wrath of God is revealed from heaven against all ungodliness and unrighteousness of men, who hold the truth in unrighteousness." (Rom. 1:18).

Back to work in the Elk's Club, one night a man came in and ordered a drink. He just stood watching me for a few minutes. I noticed him again at an after-hour joint in Campbell, Ohio. He called for me to come over as I entered the door.

"Hey, you! Come over here—I have something to ask you. Oh woman, just step to the table, please!"

I hesitated a second then walked up to the table and leaned over to hear what he had to say. He reached over and grabbed my head as if to say something in my ear, but instead, kissed me. I pulled away fast, extremely upset.

During this time in my life, men were of no interest to me. Earlier on, I had gotten myself pregnant again, from Ricky, but had lost that baby, too. I had a hysterectomy and I was yet recovering from so much heartache, hurt, and pain, I felt I was useless to any man.

Mel Baylor was the name he gave me. We passed each other that night in the gambling area where I would go to watch the men play dice. Mel approached me with an apology.

"Lady, please forgive me for my ignorance. It was your sweet look that caused me to kiss you, but I did have a question to ask. Could you take me to my hotel up in Cleveland? I must get there this morning before the maid cleans my room. I have plenty of money for her to take, and I don't want trouble. I'll make it worth your time. My partner is drunk, but you seem sober and pretty level-headed. If you don't believe my word, come let me show you."

I saw his car and his friend was lying in the backseat, drunk.

"Okay," I said, "I'll drive your car to Cleveland."

"No, mama, we better take your car and leave my buddy here to sleep. The keys are with him."

I drove my car to the motel. Just as he said, Mel showed me the money he left laying on the shelves. It was early morning and I was getting sleepy.

"Look, take the bed, and we can leave this afternoon, okay? I'll sleep in the other bed."

When I woke up, Mel was on the phone talking long distance. I took a shower and put my clothes back on. As I came back into the room, I saw that Mel was now laying in bed.

"Oh Mel, I must get back home now. It's getting late and I must work this evening. I would like to stop by Mom's to see my boys before I go to work."

Mel was so persuasive and I was so vulnerable and empty.

"Woman, get in bed with me for a few minutes and then we can leave."

Mel took his time with me. He took away the fear of never being a woman again.

I was a new person and I felt I had a sure thing going for me. This man talked and listened, taking his time with me. We walked through downtown Youngstown while we shopped and ate out. But soon came the time Mel would have to leave. We said our good-byes and kissed, then he drove off as I stood thinking, *there goes another man out of my life*. Back at work I got a lot of attention from men who normally ignored me or just ordered a drink and kept going. Now I needed wisdom and a sure foot to stand on to defend myself against the slander that came across my path. Sticks and stones may hurt my bones, but words will never hurt. So I learned body language, gestures, attitudes, and minding my own business. Yes, Ricky married another woman and Mel left town—so what?

One day the phone rang and it was for me. On the other end a lady gave me instructions about a plane ticket being held at the airport in my name. She gave the flight number and time the plane would leave, as well as its arrival time in New York City. I understood and wanted to find out who purchased the ticket, but the woman hung up. A few minutes later the phone rang again.

"Hello, woman, this is Mel. I sure miss you. I'm headed to Puerto Rico—can you join me there this weekend? Forget that job! I'll take care of you. Just make arrangements with your mother and I'll see you soon. Got to go do it, babe. Bye!"

My mother agreed to keep my boys while I traveled. All I can say to all young girls is "Dirt will settle to the bottom if you give it time.

Then you can see clearly, before you follow. Think. Follow who? To where? For what?"

Mel promised to meet me in Puerto Rico in a few days. I put so much trust in one man's word that if he would have said, "Meet me on the moon," I would have gone there to meet him. I had never been out of the United States or even west of the Mississippi River, but I was headed to Puerto Rico. Mel was not to be found, but instead a lady friend met me at the airport.

"Are you Sylvia? My name is Mary. I was told to meet you here. Mel is a close friend. He can't come just yet, but don't worry, you'll be just fine. Come with me to my apartment, and we'll call Mel."

When we arrived at Mary's apartment, I spoke with Mel on the phone. He told me he was on probation for white slavery and Puerto Rico was off limits. After we talked, his final words were, "Swim or sink!"

I was sent to handle his personal matters, seeing after his traps. His traps were for young girls whom he pimped to do a service for him. Their bodies were used to prostitute, and he would get a cut of the money they made. These girls could use the money to pay room and board, to eat, and stay well-dressed, but mainly the money belonged to the pimp.

"You're in Puerto Rico, so you must sink or swim back to the USA and also earn your own living. Your motel fees must be taken care of from here on out. Mary will teach you the ropes of how to earn that money. You're sitting on those assets, so put them to work. I won't tolerate less than seven hundred dollars a week from my traps. The girls will respect you as the wife, and they will give you my money. You have to forward it to me a week from today. Put Mary back on the phone."

Mary and I got acquainted and she told me all about this life. That evening we went out on the town; we ate and she showed me some contacts (businessmen). She assured me this was her territory and I could only work this area with her. To find my own, I would have to walk the main street, then make my own territory known with the managers, police, or whomever. I was shown the layout in the area and was told how to go about getting my own customers. I thought I would never do this ever again.

It was early morning and that night I first went out to eat, then see how this really worked for myself. The night air was much more pleasant to walk in, so I learned to sleep during the day hours, then get dressed and stroll my area seeking contacts. This is the worst and most dangerous thing any person in their right mind could do. I was constantly in jeopardy. I wouldn't advise anyone to try this; it's very degrading. If I hadn't experienced some of the things I would soon be experiencing myself, I wouldn't believe it.

I liked the atmosphere of Puerto Rico, but I hated what I found going on in the streets. As a prostitute it wasn't hard to make contacts with the men who came to do business. They paid for what they wanted. They looked for professional women who wanted to have fun with no strings attached. Some men didn't have bed relations with you, they just wanted conversation or company. These were the easy men to be with and they paid better than the dirty ones. A good prostitute dressed, looked, and acted professionally, but with some deception behind them.

I had to run once and that was because I was working with a nut. She robbed a man and told me to run for my life. Another girl had been working the life for three years and was now sixteen, looking about like twenty-five or more. She had been picked up at a bus station there in Seattle, Washington. Her pimp sent her to work with a lot of promises. One promise I learned from most of the girls, was being able to achieve an invitation to the Pimps Ball held in New York City. The girls' fantasies were about how they could earn a chance to ride in a limousine and get a date with the man who exploited them.

One of the girls had a bad disease in her body. I sent her back home after a talk, convincing her there would not be a ride in a limousine because her body was more important than any ball. I found myself sending all the girls I came in contact with, home. Yes, I became a mother with advice for each girl who came to me. One night as Nancy and I were walking, the man she thought she had killed drove his car straight toward us. I jumped out of my shoes and up and over his car, running to get clear. The streets got hot after that incident. They were not my place for business, so I was safe to go up and down the area in a cab, picking up the girls to send home. "Too much trouble out here—go back to the States!" Shielding the girls was only temporary.

My life was on the line now because I was breaking up Mel's traps. The word got out to stop me at any cost. Mel's ex-wife, also in the life, came with her girls to carry out orders to stop me. They worked by twos. This was their life and they knew how to handle the streets. I felt no fear of them, but kept my distance to watch their every move. I realized I was not in Puerto Rico for the same reason. My dates were legitimate, and I was not sending money that was so hard-earned. Our lives were already on the line, trying to swim or sink back from Puerto Rico.

One good thing did happen. The United Artists—a movie producing company followed me a week while they were filming a movie with Richard Roundtree. It was his co-worker and producer who got my attention while we sat at an outside café.

"Hey, what are you doing?" He looked at the cameras.

"We're doing a screen test to see how you look on film. We like what we see, so here, take this calling card and come see us soon."

But I lost the calling card and was never able to follow up.

Trouble followed me thereafter, and I was put out of the Sands Motel. Then after waiting for a date to pick me up at the café, I needed to use Mary's bathroom.

"Mary, let me use your bathroom and when my date comes, send him to your apartment or tell him to wait. I'll hurry, but don't forget!"

I left walking and when I reached the apartment, I saw three men standing nearby, but at a gate I also saw my date pull up in his car.

He got out and we both entered the gate, letting the men in, too. We were so caught up in ourselves that we paid the men little attention. They walked past us as I opened Mary's apartment door. Our conversation was about the crucifix about my neck.

"This? My son gave it to me for good luck. Are you interested in it or shall we go? I dare not stay here in Mary's apartment. She's nice, but not that nice. Anyhow I want some of that good shrimp." Our plans were to eat at a seafood restaurant.

Outside we headed toward the car, but as I stood waiting for my date to open the gate, a hook knife caught my chin and I had to stand on my tiptoes.

"Walk! Hurry! Move faster!" I could hear, but not see. It was very dark, yet I did vaguely see my date cross the street with another man at gunpoint. Then my body hit the pavement and a man straddled me. I was punched and my belongings were snatched from my left hand. Robbed now, I was forced on my feet and pushed to a back alley, beside which was the apartment building we had just left. First three men fondled me, then one left as the other two ripped off my clothes, pushing down my dress pants, about to further abuse me. The only thing I could say was, "Oh Lord!"

My clothes were put back on my body and the second man disappeared. I could hear a woman over the fence speak to a man who had just driven in the driveway of the apartment building and parked his car. She spoke in Spanish and was pointing in our direction. I saw the man pause, looking toward us. The one man left, while the other holding me close to him said, "Let's go!"

To my surprise, the moment I said, "Oh Lord!" a voice began to come in soft but clear. *"Tell him to let you go!"* it said.

As we walked from the back alley toward the street, I began to see a vague picture and the voice kept on speaking softly to me. *"Help is on the way."*

Like a movie, I saw my body being identified as it lay on a cold slab. Then I was flown to the United States and on to my funeral. *"Do you want to die like this?"* the voice asked. Even with the voice, the vision, because the man was still holding on, I could hardly walk. My legs trembled as he dragged me out of that alley. He forced me to walk close to his side.

I whispered, "Let me go!"

As he turned, he answered, "No! You see my face, I kill you. Take me to your car!" He held on tightly to his gun.

How absolute is God and what He says He'll do, I learned that night. Help did come. Mary was riding in a car that drove up into the driveway. She rolled her window down from the backseat.

"Hey man, you know her. Is she your friend? She's mine, too. She has my keys! Let her go!"

By now Mary had opened the door and with a purse, she wrapped the straps around her right hand as she pulled his gun out of his pants. Mary swung her purse, knocking the gun to the ground. I heard Mary say, "Break loose and run!"

I broke away as the man reached down for his gun which had headed toward a sewage hole.

"Feet, don't fail me now!" I ran until I reached the lights of Main Street and summoned a policeman who walked the area.

"Sir, I was robbed by three men! They took my date off to kill him! Please come to the next street, a block away, on Juain Street."

The police came and I stood in the place I had been accosted.

"Madam, what do you want me to do? There are many cases like this, but you seem to be okay. Go back to your motel and when I hear of anything, I'll notify you. Go, please!"

In a cab on my way back to the motel, I saw a man sitting on the drugstore steps, trying to put my crucifix around his neck. I told the cab driver to stop by the policeman who stood on the next corner.

"Sir, there is one of the men sitting on the drugstore steps." I pointed toward the area. He told me to meet him there in a few minutes.

By the time we drove around the block, we met up with the policeman. I got out of the cab and walked over slowly, trying to hear what was being said. All I could see was the man shaking his head 'no' to each question. The policeman turned and said, "This man doesn't know about you or what happened. So we…"

I interrupted, "He has my crucifix in his hand!"

The policeman spoke in Spanish. "Let me see what's in your hand!"

The man jumped up and ran like a rabbit as the officer shot out after him, chasing him with his walkie-talkie in his hands, calling for backup.

At the end of the street all sorts of men—police, detectives, and undercover officers, seemed to come from nowhere. By the time I reached the action, they had tackled the man to the ground and emptied his pockets, finding all my belongings.

"Are these your things? They look like the items you described stolen from you."

They were, and he also had my money, which was tucked in a hard pack of cigarettes.

"Yes, they're mine."

With this I was taken to the police station to press charges.

All the families of the captured men had come and were mad. As I got out of the police car, they were shouting obscenities.

"You walk close to me. You understand why they're are angry at you, don't you?" the detective asked.

I grabbed the detective's arm and we entered the judge's quarters. At first I was not going to press charges until I heard and saw the reason why I should.

"Madam, these men have killed several women since February. Look at these pictures of how we found each of them. Don't feel sorry or afraid. We'll look after you. Just write the account of what happened and sign the papers. You can't leave Puerto Rico until this is all over or until we follow up on this case."

I hurried and wrote out what happened, then signed the papers so I could get out of Puerto Rico fast.

A few days later, I was getting dressed for the evening when one of the girls came to visit me in my motel room. She asked if I would come up the hall and talk with some of Mel's girls who had not sent in their money. I told her I would, after my shower, and sent her to see if the time for me to come was good for everyone. I had stepped into the bathroom and showered, then put on my wig, which had my money pinned inside. While I looked into the mirror, I could see one of my girls who had joined up with Mel's girls. They had come from Hawaii to investigate me. The girl once was Mel's wife who worked as I was supposed to. She and her girls were sent to find out why I wasn't doing my job—seeing to Mel's money—to be sent to him each week. As I placed the wig on my head, looking in the mirror, I could see the girl riffling through my suitcase and the pillow on my bed, trying to find my money.

You see, if she did rob me, I would be at their mercy and would have to do the things I detested. I could not ever let them get the jump on me; I had to stay in control or be messed up like so many other girls. Figuring what was about to happen, I waited for the girl to leave.

"Tell the girls I'll see them as soon as I put my clothes on. Give me about ten minutes—just tell them ten minutes."

I watched her smooth out my bedding and walk toward the door. "Okay, see you in a few."

She closed the door and I stepped out of the bathroom, picked up my suitcase, and left right behind her, taking the stairway down and hailing a cab. "Take me to the airport!"

After arriving at the LaGuardia Airport, I took another cab to the city of New York.

"Take me to the President's Hotel on Forty-third Street."

I was dressed to the max wearing my sunglasses. The cabby thought I was a foreigner and instead of driving me to the hotel, he headed toward the tunnel that goes to New Jersey.

"Stop right over there, I've got to get some cigarettes."

He stopped at a newsstand and I got out with my belongings. Outside the cab, with the door still open, I said, "Hey, I live in this city. What did you think you were doing?" I slammed the door and stepped out into the street to wave another cab down. "Take me uptown."

Mel had left word I should never come to the city without permission. I felt as much a woman as he was a man. Marcus, his best friend, had been to Puerto Rico and threatened me with his gun. This was a deadly mistake on Marcus's part, to break street rules. A pimp could not mess with another pimp's woman. Since I dared to tell Mel what Marcus had done to me with his gun, how dare he tell me not to come to the city! Hey, I played in the city when I lived upstate.

I knocked at his apartment door.

"Who is it?" said a weak voice.

"Mel, it's Sylvia. May I come in? We have things to talk about, something very important."

This handsome man stood looking me over. "Come in. It had better be good, or your assets belong to me!"

While we talked, there was a knock at the door.

"Sylvia, sit still. Let me see who is at the door first."

Mel opened the door, and a woman dressed in an airline steward's outfit stepped inside. I barely heard her say, "It was a breeze. Easy, too," as she handed him a package.

In the package were diamonds which I later found out, had been stolen. While I continued to talk, Mel took my hand and put a diamond ring on my ring finger.

"Girl, let me marry you tomorrow?" he said.

Mel liked me because I didn't drink or do drugs like some of the other girls. It would have been foolish of me to even try drugs or alcohol because my body could not tolerate such junk. Drugs deaden the conscious mind. Mel saw in me a business prospect, but it wouldn't work, for my direction in life was far from the way he would have taken me had I not left him. Oh, I was offered diamonds, beautiful homes, and many other fineries, but none of those things excited me.

The next day we drove up to Boston, Massachusetts. There we searched for Mel's stolen car. The doggy gets dogged! There were times when I had a strong sense of perception and could discern many things. I told Mel exactly where he could find his car. I never was in Boston before, so Mel tested me.

"You're so smart, take me to my car."

I began to direct him when to go left or make a right and we came right to his car.

"Mel, look, there goes your car!"

Sure enough, the car passed by. It had been stolen by one of Mel's girls and we followed it to a jamming point. I lost a beautiful coat running out, by leaving it all behind because there was a shootout and I got out.

Mel caught up with me, then we drove out of town to meet with a few co-workers who dabbled in the same business Mel did—women! When we stopped, there were two Rolls Royces. One man approached our car, holding a black cane with diamonds on the top. They demonstrated on each other, like shadow boxing, pointing the canes at each other. The canes were weapons of some sort. Another man took a minute to look in the backseat where I sat.

"Hey man, look what I see, a pretty fine girl. Mel, is that your number one girl? Let's make an exchange—I like what I see!"

I sat still, not saying a word.

"Look man, I just want my car, but you can't have this girl. She's all mine and not for sale, just give me my car!" he said seriously. Mel turned to me.

"Sylvia, take this rented car back to New York City and park it on the street near the hotel. Wait there for me, I'm bringing company with me, so don't get jealous or do a dumb thing."

Mel came to the hotel the next afternoon with another woman. After meeting the girl, I stayed my distance. That evening we would go out to make a few dollars, but I was so determined and had a streak of stubbornness in me. So I sat at Nathan's at Forty-second Street, ate, and watched the different girls *handle* the area—which was swarming with action. I watched and made up in my mind this was not for me, as I had said long before. At first chance I would go back home. I would not let Mel or his other women run my life.

In the hotel room late that night, there was a big argument. The girls from Hawaii by way of Puerto Rico had come to New York and talked with Mel, telling him I was not doing my part and they wanted him to do something about the matter. It turned out we would all go work the streets together the following evening and bring our money to Mel. All his women slept over in the hotel room that night. That afternoon we began to dress for the evening out, taking baths, fixing our hair, and dolling up for the night's work. I was the last to get ready and stepped out to take most of my clothes to a dry cleaner. I needed time for myself for a few minutes, to think.

Food was not a must in this life, but we did order from a nearby restaurant. It was nearly eight o'clock.

"Okay, girls, time to get to work. Go out by twos. Who will go first?"

I was getting my food, so I spoke up and said, "I'll go with Dawn."

But she refused and so did the others. So I kept eating while Mel sent them out. It was nearing nine-thirty when one of the couples came back to check things out.

"Mel, where is Sylvia? She thinks she is a smart cookie, but we girls are going to put her in space soon! We're just waiting to get her!"

After she left, Mel told me to get in bed and rest. I did, knowing anything could happen from here on out. Mel lay next to me and we talked things out. He told me how he felt about the whole matter, of how my life could be snuffed out by one of the girls. I assured him I knew the danger I was in now, that I was not out for working the streets. The phone rang, and Mel picked it up.

"What do you mean, all the girls are in jail?"

They each had been picked up and needed to be bailed out. This cost a pimp money.

The following morning after Mel posted bail, the girls came and questioned me.

"Listen, girls, I stood on the bus stop and watched you dummies get picked up by the paddy wagon. How did all of you end up in jail? Seems that one or two, but six? Someone wasn't smart. Why didn't any of you take a bus uptown until it was clear?"

That evening we would try it again, but I went to Nathan's and called Cohen's old phone number. To my surprise, he answered the phone.

"Cohen, come get me out of this mess. I'm in trouble!" I sat at the window at Nathan's and waited for Cohen to come.

"Stay put, I'll be right there!" was Cohen's response.

I thought how it was going to be leaving Mel, but I realized I wanted my life and my children, and I knew this was the best decision to make.

Cohen parked outside where I could see him. I waved to him to come beside me. I told him what was going down.

"Walk to the car and I'll follow you. I'll be your final date."

To look back would have been a big mistake. I left some valuable items, but they could not pay for my life. I made a clean break.

In the car we headed upstate to Ossinging, New York.

"Cohen, will you marry me? I've got to get out of this life. I mean, really get married in June, after I get home and see my boys."

Cohen laughed, but said, "If that's what you want."

Chapter 14

June 2, 1974 came fast. I took my car to the corner of Oakhill and Warren Avenue, to have the car brakes checked. The station attendant told me what I needed was "Salvation!" I heard him tell me things that had been said to me about Jesus. Jerome had told me first, but I had my own mind made up. That afternoon, the boys and I would travel to Ossinging, New York. Who needed Jesus anyhow? I did, but first…?

My wedding dress had been given to me by Mrs. Hillelson. She also gave me some advice.

"Don't marry that Cohen man, but let us marry you into the Jewish religion first." She guaranteed me an inheritance, but I lacked understanding, so I declined. The next day we reached Ossinging in time for the wedding. After the wedding we packed the car and headed toward Youngstown, Ohio. It wasn't long before Cohen expressed his jealousy.

"Syl, let's move to Cleveland. I'll find work there since General Motors turned down my application for a transfer."

We found an apartment in Cleveland and moved. Cohen was good at painting so we sought work painting homes. I also found a barmaid position on Lee Road. Painting homes was a bit too much. For Cohen, we found a way for him to join the Painter's Union. *"Think it, then do it!"* was our attitude. Our car would carry the ladders, and we would purchase order sheets to advertise our business by passing out fliers. In order for him to do interior work, we sent him to school to learn how to improve his wallpapering abilities, then Cohen found work with a large painting company. Our income was set for good now.

September started out with my sister Marva telling me she had cancer. Marva would worry me by way of my mother.

"Sylvia, come see about your sister. She wants to see you."

"What can I do, Mom?" But something kept pulling at me. *"Go see your sister!"*

Busy with the children in school, my husband, and work, intertwining one with another, I tried hard to ignore the fact my sister was sick unto death. To get rid of that tension, I drove down one evening to see her. Marva told me how she had driven with her husband to California.

"Those cigars my husband smoked made me so sick, but I could not tell him. Then on top of that, on my job, I mixed two chemicals together, bleach and ammonia. The gases hit me in the face and I passed out. Now the cancer is in my pancreas and lungs. Promise you'll see after my children, please!"

I went back home and tried not to think about the condition my sister was in. What could I do anyhow? The harder I pushed it behind, the more it stood before me. As I lay on the couch one evening, something came over me. *"Go to your sister, now!"* I got up and drove straight to her hospital and stood there at her bedside.

"Marva, do you need me?"

"Sylvia, please ask my company out, I must use the bathroom." I turned and asked her husband Ralph and those he was talking with, to leave the room. I then helped my sister out of bed and led her to the bathroom. I went to straighten out her bedding, and the bright red blood on her sheet told me she was seriously ill. I assisted my sister back to her bed.

"Marva, would you like it if I stayed overnight with you?"

Of course she said, "Yes!"

Then I went to the nurse's station. "May I stay overnight with my sister?"

The nurse was glad I asked. "Are you her sister? It was thought that someone should stay. You know her condition is grave?"

Ralph was satisfied that I would stay, too. When leaving he stopped to say, "If you need me, just call. I'll come right over." He spoke slowly as I took a seat at the foot of her bed and watched the nurse work with my sister changing her bed, giving her a shot and fixing her I.V.'s. They were busy bringing in a new patient, and after making that patient comfortable, they turned to me. "What can we do to make you comfortable? Here's a blanket, and coffee is up in the nurse's station."

The light went out and Marva began to talk, more than she had talked to me for a long time. Marva had a quiet spirit, and she usually had very little to say.

"Sylvia, are you okay? Are you comfortable sitting there like that? The doctors say I will get knots on my neck—did you see any? Will I lose my voice? Can you hear me?"

Marva kept this up for two hours. Then about one-thirty, my sister fell off to sleep. As I watched, it appeared her eyes sank to the back of her head. But what was so strange was, I fell into a trance. What I saw was foreign to me. A soft, cloud-like form of fog crept along the floor, into the room. It was the Angel of Death, coming to take my sister. I watched until I blinked my eyes, then I couldn't see it as it reached her bed.

Marva spoke up. "Sylvia, my hour has come. Call Ralph!"

We waited for my brother-in-law to arrive. Marva weakly started asking questions.

"Could you do me a favor? Ask your God to spare me just one more day so I can see my children before I leave this place. Also ask Him to let me live. Tell Him I'll serve Him daily with my whole heart, soul, and mind. Please, Sylvia, do this. You know Him!"

How dare she make such a strong request and say I know Him?

"Marva, I don't know this God you are talking about, but I will go and pray when Ralph comes. Will that make you feel better?" I asked.

She nodded.

It was early morning when Ralph stepped in the room. He took a seat next to my sister and held her hands. I headed down to the chapel of St. Elizabeth Hospital. There I opened the door and spoke in my thoughts: *Lord, I come just as I am; humble as I know how. Please accept me and my prayer.* I then knelt at the altar, but before I could say a word, I heard an audible voice, say, "SYLVIA! IT'S NOT YOUR WILL, BUT MINE WILL BE DONE!" I said nothing but got up and went to tell Ralph I would be at home resting. Marva instructed me to bring her children back.

I slept in my sister's home. After four hours of rest, I woke to Marva's voice, which had traveled up to where I slept, calling me as if she were right downstairs. I jumped up, dazed, forgetting she was still in the hospital. I stood at the top of the stairway. "Yes, Marva!" I yelled, then I realized where I was.

Vincent, her oldest son, Diane, her oldest daughter; and Kathy arrived at the hospital with me. Andrea, her two-year-old, was too young to come into her mother's room. I told Diane to let him stay with his father. As we entered, Marva began to name each child as they walked closer to their mother's bedside.

"Where is my baby? Come closer, kids," my sister said with outstretched hands.

I couldn't bear to watch so I stepped out into the hall where my brother and sister from out of town now waited. Tears flowed, then each child came out of the room. I came back in the room now. Vincent sat in a chair and took her hand as I stood on the other side. As I looked out the large window at the horizon, I realized how big God was. This earth belongs to Him, as do all we, His little ones. I'm just a spot of dust to compare this mighty God. He is in control of everything. He never sleeps or slumbers. Now here I stand looking death straight in the face. Even if I knew how to rebuke death, I had no authority to do so. My sister, looking up to the ceiling, said, "Vincent!" That was her final word. I placed my hands over her eyes, closing them.

One of Marva's requests was to dress her to make her look presentable. "Fix my hair, put me in a green dress, and don't forget to place shoes on my feet. I may want to walk around Heaven all day. Do you think I'll make Heaven?" These were some of her requests. At the funeral home, I dressed Marva and put on her makeup and placed her shoes on. *Am I ready for Heaven?* It was a sincere thought. We buried my sister the last Friday of October, 1974.

That Sunday, November 3rd, I went to the Pentecostal Church just to say, "Thank you, Lord!" because many of the ministers there took the time to visit and pray for my sister's recovery. The pastor was preaching the sermon, "Yielding to the Spirit." The message pulled me down to the altar and there I was asked, "Have you been baptized in the name of Jesus?"

Of course I said "No!" That little soft voice spoke out and overruled my ignorant desires. *"Yes! Take me to the water! What harm could a little water do?"* November 3rd, 1974, I was baptized in Jesus's name. I had no idea that to be baptized would wash away my sinful body, thus make me a new creation. And as I stood outside the church, everything around me was a glazed color of amber. The blood of Jesus had stained my eyes.

"For as much then as Christ hath suffered for us in the flesh, arm yourselves likewise with the same mind; for he that hath suffered in the flesh hath ceased from sin." (1 Pet. 4:1)

"Humble, then; Casting all your care upon him; for he careth for you." (1 Pet. 5:6-7).

November 3rd, I was baptized and felt strange leaving Youngstown driving back to my home in Cleveland Heights. The first thing I did was call my neighbor and told her what I did. I made mention of the fact I wanted to attend a church in Cleveland because it was sixty miles to go back east to Youngstown. She invited me to her church, and that following Sunday, I went with her.

This was not going to work. I felt it right away, but what it was exactly, I really could not put my finger on. The pastor of that church, the Church of God in Christ, asked for all new members to come to the front for the right hand of fellowship and candidates for baptism. I stood with the others, but heard that soft voice say, *"Leave this place!"* I went through the motions, as the pastor and his laymen passed by each of us to shake our hands. But in my heart I knew this was not right. I didn't want to hurt my neighbor, so I kept quiet.

We went back Sunday, November 17th. I dressed my children and we attended a church in Youngstown, the Pentacostal Church. It was good, but I had to go home after visiting my mother. On our way home as I drove down Hillman Street, the soft small voice said, *"I have a surprise for you—go to Pentacostal's Church."* My car wheels turned down Delason as if I had no control.

"Okay, boys we are going back to church. There's a surprise for me."

The people were standing giving testimonies. At first, out of ignorance, I found them to be funny until I heard, "You praise me!"

I said, "No!" All of a sudden, lightning came from where, I can't say, but it hit me on the derriere. The jolt sent me out of my seat, and it shook me, saying, "YOU PRAISE ME!" My head shook, my eyes rolled, and I had no control. When I would try to sit down, I would come flying out of my seat as if it was hot. This went on until I began to yield and said, "Yes, Lord! Yes, Lord!"

A young girl from the choir came over to me. "You must go to the upper room. God wants to fill you with his power." I tried to keep still, but the Spirit was all about me. Just at the thought of NO, the spirit would shake me. "Okay, I'll go," I said.

The door was opened to the upper room, and the girl ushered me into the room. "Now you praise him! Say HALLELUJAH! Say it! God's going to fill you now. That's it, there He is. Say it, say it!"

So much power filled the room until the girl was moving listlessly, all over, like tissue paper. A golden bright light filled the room and I could see Jesus walking over to me. My eyes were closed, but I could see Him there on the cross, then in a garden. He came close, then all I could see were His feet. God poured out his power on my head. We talked and I knew I had received the power of the Holy Ghost. He told me. The girl took me out afterwards, and I met the pastor on his way to his office. At that time he was a District Elder.

I got it! I got it! Something about the Holy Ghost I can't explain, but I got it! Driving on my way back home, I asked the question, "What is this marvelous thing you have done to me?" At home, God instructed me to open that dusty Bible. When I laid the Bible on the dining room table, it opened to the Book of Acts. I knew nothing about the books of the Bible outside of Psalms 23, but I read where my eyes led me. Acts 2:1.

"And when the day of Pentecost was fully come, they were all with one accord in one place, and suddenly there came a sound from heaven like a rushing mighty wind, and it filled all the house where they were sitting, and there appeared unto them cloven tongues as of fire, and it sat upon each of them. And they were all filled with the Holy Ghost, and began to speak with other tongues, as the SPIRIT gave them utterance. God spoke, "I will lead and guide you, into all truth."

I started school to learn secretarial skills. It seemed everyone looked at me so strangely.

"Girl, what happened to you? Did you see a ghost?"

I looked like a ghost myself, and during break, I told those who had interest, what happened. The next day at lunchtime one of the students questioned me.

"How are you going to tell me you got the Holy Ghost? I, too, have the Holy Ghost, and I would not dare smoke a cigarette."

She was right, but out of ignorance and with no proper teaching, I had not given myself time to attend any Bible classes as of yet. I was a babe in Christ and was polluting my temple with detestable things. It's through a process of time that God would and still does work on my temple. I couldn't understand—each time I would light up a cigarette, it would burn out before I could get a puff. So that Wednesday evening after my family all went out, I sat down to have a good smoke. With my feet propped up on the coffee table, I sat on the couch with my fresh pack of Pall Malls. As I pulled one cigarette out of the pack, I could hear, *"Don't smoke that cigarette!"* Paying no attention, I lit it and took a drag. To my surprise, the smoke turned into mortar in my mouth. I was choked to the point of not being able to breathe. In my mind, I communicated with the voice.

"If you let this out, I won't smoke ever again, please..." The smoke came out into a perfect smoke ring and vanished into thin air. From that day on, I haven't smoked, nor have I the desire to.

My next problem would be my husband. "Sylvia, go get me a pack of cigarettes from the store?" Seems like I had just said no, completely "No!" The Spirit would teach me to resist the works of the devil. My husband would become my adversary.

"You have been to that church and got the Ghost. Now you're a trader." Cohen began to hate the sight of me. For a moment we did try to reason, but..? The question was, why did he fight me so hard?

One morning I awakened from a dream. I dreamt Cohen and I were arguing and he jumped at me, turning into a large snake, and bit my thigh. I woke up finding his hand laying on my thigh where in the dream, he had bit me. Looking at his body in the blanket, it held the shape of that large snake I had just seen in my dream. I got out of bed and headed to the bathroom where Cohen had gone just before me. There I found the bath water I had run the night before, turned red. Cohen had thrown my Bible in the tub, and the red letters caused this effect.

The Lord began to work with me and teach me things I should not do. Makeup had always been a pleasure for me to wear, so this would be hard to break from doing. I had just won the title, "Miss Auto Rama, 1974." I was a model with the Barbizon Modeling School in Cleveland. I earned a trip to New York to do a script on a daytime program. Also, I was a Mary Kay consultant. One morning as I applied my cosmetics, my cheeks turned orange. My fake eyelashes, glue and all, went into my eyes, turning them bloodshot. Then the lipstick made my lips look very large. *"Take it off!"* I heard that voice, so I wiped my face clean. I wanted to be obedient, and I would learn I was a new creature of Christ, behold old things are passed away. For me, I had to be changed and Jesus knew my heart. It would all be done in a process of time. God was working on my temple. Coming out of the old into the new, I would have to make a difference. I could not be the same Sylvia who did as I so pleased. My outer appearance had to look like my inner. I would be completely turned around. Bible class would teach me more.

I changed so much that one day my husband told me, "If I wanted a holy woman, I would have married one. Look at you, you're a mess."

The Holy Spirit began to use me. My neighbor, my mother, my friends, and others came to know Jesus and His plan of salvation. As for my husband, I left him after he tried to burn me with the Bible. I hungered and thirsted for righteousness, anything but the lifestyle I had lived. Day and night I read the wonderful word of God.

I could not keep up with the latest styles and had to shop in places I could afford, plus I had begun to gain weight. I went from a size seven to a size fourteen, it seemed, overnight. But I wanted more of Jesus than anything.

Graduate Of Modeling School

Sylvia Cohen formerly of Youngstown, graduate of Barbizon Modeling School of Cleveland, Crowned Miss Auto Rama 1974 in Cleveland's Public Hall, Hostess to the Lion Club convention at Sheraton Inn in Cleveland, she has cut commercials in Muscle Shoals Ala. for Bl ack Products.

Ms. Cohen will direct and model for the E.T.C.'s Club here at Cherry's Top of the Mall in the Eastwood Mall. To help introduce hidden models. The models will be Debbie Wood, Sally Haynes, Lafawn Carter, Dianne Cameron, Kevin Singleton Lawence, Tyrone Williams of Cleveland, Wilson Nadel.

Commentator will be Rosetta Bennett, produced by B.J. Tate. For further information Call 747-6064 or 744-2273.

A PAIR OF HOT PANTS and the simple things of Mother Nature together makes Miss Autorama breathtaking. Miss Sylvia Cohen was crowned Miss Autorama at the Cleveland Public Hall during annual auto show last week. Miss Cohen, a Leo, who hopes to find a career in modeling, enjoys bowling, swimming, singing, and painting. Vital statistics are 34-24-37, which stacks up and is "outa sight." (Photo by Arthur St. Clair)

Chapter 15

I soon moved back to Youngstown on Kenmore Street and began to work at the Strauss Department Store. It was early spring and the church would go on a fast. To fast, we would deny ourselves worldly pleasures and devote ourselves to the Spirit. We gave up worldly pleasures like television, eating three meals a day, and if married, the pleasure of being intimate with one's husband or wife. The first two days we would eat one meal. On the third day, we weren't allowed to eat or drink and continued the complete fast for three days, so we could be completely consecrated to God. The church doors were opened for six a.m., eleven a.m., and seven o'clock prayer services as well as Bible class twice daily. Friday we broke our fast and that evening took Holy Communion.

This move to Youngstown was good for my soul. I grew closer to God during these communions. I now spent all my time in church. My soul was delighted. My children, too, enjoyed seeing me happy for once and they hardly gave me any trouble attending church. They also found it was the right move to make. After seeing Mom go through so much, they never said anything negative. They would join me on these fast days, which made it easier. But I never forced them—it was their choice to do so. It was the best for us all.

During my first fast, I was on my knees praying when I felt a splash of cool water hit my face. Ministering angels had come to help me at my lowest point. Being without water or food brings your body down, but the spirit will rise up. The next morning as I lay in my bed, I heard that voice say, *"Look!"* I was weak, but I looked out the northwest window where I saw a silhouette of a city sitting on a bed of clouds coming down out of heaven. The angels were singing and rays of gold covered the background. It was beautiful. Today the fast would be over so I could ask for most anything and get it. I asked for a large beef tomato and drove to the flea market where I was given a bushel basket of beef tomatoes just by asking. What a lesson to learn! In God's plan of salvation there are many avenues of blessings. The Word of God says it like this: If you ask for a fish, would He will give you a stone?

I learned there was power in the tongue. So I had to be watchful of how and what I spoke. For thirty-two years, I said and did as I pleased, yet to this day I still learn God has the first and final say over any matter.

For from within, out of the heart of man, proceed evil thoughts, adulteries, fornications, murders, thefts, covetousness, wickedness, deceit, lasciviousness, an evil eye, blasphemy, pride, and foolishness. All these evil things come from within and defile the man (Mark 7:21,22).

So I would reconcile unto my husband, realizing I was not going to win him to Christ by separating from him. He asked for me to forgive him and come back home. This I did and for a moment, he almost crossed over into salvation.

Bishop C. Watkins would become my pastor while in Cleveland. I also learned more about serving in the church. I became a pastor's aide. Bishop was so mature and endured many experiences. He taught us a different view in walking with the Lord and called all his children and threatened anyone who intended to harm our walk while God worked on our perfection. Most of my understanding came from the Scriptures.

Nevertheless, "the foundation of God standeth sure. Having this seal, the Lord knoweth them that are his; and let everyone that nameth the name of Christ depart from iniquity… But in a great house there are not only vessels of gold and of silver, but also of wood and of earth; and some of honor, and some of dishonor…" (1 Tim. 2:20,21).

He saw us all as children of God, some to honor and some to dishonor, some as wood and stubble and some as gold, but all belonged to the higher power of God. One example I recall was a young girl who said she had the Holy Ghost. But we knew different because she never received it while tarrying for it. She felt the power and spoke with stammering lips, but never did she speak with other tongue, a foreign language which can be interpreted by a person of that native tongue, be it Spanish, Japanese, or German. There are over 164 languages.

The Bishop would say, "Leave her alone, she acts more Christianized than some of you."

One Sunday while singing in the choir, God filled her with the Holy Ghost. That evening she testified, "I thought I had the Holy

Spirit, but now I know without a doubt, I got it!" The church went up in a shout. This is how the Bishop felt: "Leave them alone, and let God do the judging. He can handle them better. Stay in your own place, in which God called you."

Earrings, makeup, and a way to dress—he was for it all to be a Godly right. But we, as parishioners, could not undress nor dress anyone.

"If the Word don't condemn you, neither do I," Bishop Watkins would often say. He used all the talents in the church, for he believed they were gifts sent for the works of the church for them to edify the church.

I became a minister by acknowledging my call after telling Bishop Watkins of the experience I had after being admitted to the St. Luke's Hospital. I had a blood clot in my kidney which needed to be drained out. Then after that, my gallbladder failed and surgery was performed. I was very sick. I also had pneumonia because I had been placed under the air conditioning duct while recovering from the operation. I had come out of the recovery room and placed back in my private room that evening to be made comfortable for the night.

I dreamt a girl was walking on to a plank to board a ship which had come to dock in the Cleveland Bay, on Lake Erie. In that dream, a voice said, *"Halt! Your time has not come."* I was awakened to the nurses and doctors administering medication for my condition. After applying some oxygen and being given a few shots, I lay resting quietly. Then I heard angels singing a song I learned while attending Sunday School as a young girl.

"Jesus loves me, this I know, for the Bible tells me so. Little ones to him belong, they are weak, but He is strong. Yes, Jesus loves me, yes Jesus loves me, yes Jesus loves me, for the Bible tells me so."

These angels entered my room through a window I had been looking out. They filled the room, lining up around my bed and pausing for a moment, their heads turned toward the same window. I did too, and saw Jesus walk into my room. He spoke.

"Sylvia, go tell my people: in the beginning was God!"

I could not describe how the angels looked: neither could I say how God looked, but I saw Him. He moved to my back and nodded His head to one angel. A Bible was placed in His hand, then He opened up my back and laid the Bible in my back. "Tell the people: in the beginning was the Word!" He then exited my window.

That next morning I called the Bishop and told him what I had experienced.

"What took you so long? I'll talk with you later about what you should do next," was his response.

On March 11, 1979, I preached my first sermon: "Imagination of Thought/A Piercing View, from the Book of Genesis, 6:5." On my thirty-ninth birthday, July 5th, I received my ministering licenses. Soon I would come to understand the Scriptures.

"For a great door, and effectual, is opened unto me, and there are many adversaries" (1 Cor. 16:9).

My husband was one of my first adversaries. He spit in my face. He set my Bible on fire, with intention of setting me ablaze. He stopped his obligations and denied the care for me. Finally, a judge ordered we divorce because he choked Marvin nearly to death. We divorced in November of 1979 and I took on a job with the Ross family was terminated. She replaced me while I was sick in St. Luke's Hospital. Just before the divorce I took another job with the Millikins as Mrs. Millikin's personal maid. They were elderly and held great respect for life. Living with them taught me people are people world round. There are qualities and quantities. Also I learned a chicken is a chicken as cotton is cotton. We all must eat, sleep, and have basic desires.

I moved back to Youngstown for a short while before going to California. The break-up with my husband caused me to drift, taking on most live-in jobs. I hated that we made marriage vows and could not live them out.

Chapter 16

It was while in California for a duration of five months that I attended Bishop McMurry's church. The day I arrived in California, my aunt told me she could not take me anyplace, but gave me the keys to one of her cars. I have always been good at following road maps and believe it came mostly from growing up and hiking in a wooded area at my birth place. With that car I found my way to Bishop McMurry's church and other places.

That following Sunday I drove to Los Angeles to church, and from that day on, traveled all over the State of California. Bishop McMurry pulled out the hidden gifts in me after I was put on the Ministerial team. Training was a part of my development. We were taught the priestly duties: baptize, laying on of hands, and how to conduct communion. I attended school and preached in church as well as out in the streets. I reached the apex of my spiritual life. The anointing was high, and those in opposition of Christ, pressed hard against me.

My next job would be a live-in position caring for an elderly lady in her son and daughter-in-law's home. A car was at my disposal for shopping and to take the lady to the doctor. I cleaned, shopped, and cooked. On weekends I was free to go and do as I wished. Some Wednesdays, I would go clean their office and made a few extra dollars. But I hardly spent my earnings because everything was provided for me.

One day while praying just before going to bed, I prayed about everyone who came to my mind, asking, "Lord, am I in you will?" All of a sudden the room shook. I got up and climbed into my bed, and the room stopped shaking. *Um*, I thought, *maybe it was an earthquake.* That morning while attending to some chores, I asked, "Did you feel that earthquake last night?"

"What earthquake? We didn't have an earthquake!" The son, his wife, and Grandma all looked at me puzzled.

That day I would take my lunch break and walk up into the mountain area. I sat and talked to God as I did when I was just a little girl. He showed me things in the Spirit which to this day I cannot explain, but I knew I was there on the mountain with Him. It was beautiful up there looking over L.A.

That night I would kneel and pray again, but this time I asked, "Lord, am I in your will?" The room shook so hard I was sure this was a big quake. I began to realize again this was not an earthquake, but God telling me something. I jumped into bed and covered my head. The next morning I dared not ask anyone about last night. While ironing, the phone rang, and it was for me. My lawyer had called for me to come home and sign papers concerning my home back in Cleveland, Ohio, and to finalize the divorce agreement. As I placed the phone back on the receiver, I pondered in my mind about the room shaking. God was allowing me to experience the sensation of His power and to assure me. He heard my prayer and had control of my life.

The long ride home on the Greyhound bus gave me time to think of what to do after I arrived in Cleveland. I called my lawyer and we agreed to meet at the courthouse the next day. I went to another agency and applied for another live-in position, only temporarily, for I had told the staff in California I would return. My plans were not God's plan. The people for whom I worked in Los Angeles were about to tell me they were making a move back east and could no longer employ me. I used their reference and was hired in Cleveland on the spot. The purpose of coming to see this lawyer was only to settle out of court who would get the house and to see if Cohen was going to pay alimony. The next morning I called my lawyer's office.

"Oh, Mrs. Cohen, the lawyer passed away suddenly last night during his supper. Please call back in a few weeks. Another lawyer will cover your case."

My lawyer dropped dead and so did my case. I lost everything but my mind. I even lost my freedom, after I took a line-in job that was confining—so much so I felt like leaving without notice, but I had no car.

My mother had to come up to Cleveland and rescue me from that job. I had no way out of those woods, and they held me for weeks, working without any relief or days off. I left without pay.

"Mom, just come get me out of here, now!" I whispered on the phone.

Returning home to Youngstown was a relief. I again started attending the only thing left me, the Pentecostal Church. Taking my position as one of the ministers, I devoted my time to the things pertaining to the work of God.

Finally, I found an apartment in the Senior Citizen's Apartment complex. It was the best thing I could do at the time. I was tired and weary as I was from the last job. They tried to work me to death. Not like in California, where I only had to watch the little grandma and her dog, so baby-sitting was easy. But a man's work of scrubbing floors and washing windows was too much for me to handle. My ailments were also a hindrance.

I started back to school at Youngstown State University while attending church, and keeping my apartment was all I could manage to do. For some reason I could hardly make school and barely kept my apartment clean for inspection. But I could regain my footsteps and shut out the negative things by praising God for the good He had done for me. Not knowing I was very sick in my body, it became very hard just to carry my books up and down Wick Avenue, coming and going to school. I was becoming seriously ill and while at church one evening, I could hardly breathe. I was taken to the hospital, St. Elizabeth's on the north side and admitted. I would be forced to drop my schooling.

At St. Elizabeth's Hospital I was asked to leave because my insurance would no longer cover my stay. Calling Dr. Perry who had taken care of me for other ailments. He'd let me know what steps I should take from there. A few days later I was admitted into the Southside Hospital and surgery was my next trial. I had to undergo a spleenectomy, and during this operation, four pints of the wrong type of blood were administered to me. With God and the hands of my surgeon, I survived. It was a battle to recover from that operation, but thanks to Dr. Perry, a prominent surgeon in the area, and the saints of God and God's mercy, I pulled through.

Within that year I sought a lawyer. He said I was one day too late, that I no longer had a case. This lawyer never tried to represent me, to carry out his duties. Dr. Perry, within that year had set my records aside in his office waiting for a call from my lawyer—which never came.

My body went through a series of ailments, and several times I had to be readmitted. Today my soul looks back and wonders how I came out not being brain dead or paralyzed. Even when I applied for my disability, the judge could not believe me as I stood before him during a hearing. I had to take my case with another lawyer to the higher courts. This was an excellent lawyer, as he exhibited A, B, C, and D, showing how the wrong blood was given. During that hearing the judge ordered both my lawyer and I out of his courtroom saying, "Look at her, you and your client, get out." The Supreme Court overruled and granted me my disability. Even today, looking at me, you'd never know I had been sick.

Chapter 17

Samuel Whittenburg was an older man I'd met in church. He had been a friend of the family for years. He had lived next door to my mother and knew my uncles since his childhood. This man took to calling me every day to make sure I was okay when he found out who my family was. If I was sick, I couldn't be as long as he was around.

"Girl, let's go out to eat. Get your mother and we can travel. I like going places, don't you?"

This would never end, not with Sam. It came to a time he needed help for himself and his doctor suggested I move into his home to care for him. Sam was so happy the day I agreed and settled there in his home to be a help for him.

We also did a great deal of traveling. Sam, Joan, my friend from church, and I. If the car carried us, we traveled—Miami, Florida, New Orleans, L.A., New York—name it. If we had gas and money, we traveled. Sometimes Sam slept in the car while we girls slept comfortably in a motel. Then at times we would put Sam in the room with us, and he slept in the bathroom or on a cot. But we slept in some of the finest hotels in the United States. We ate at some of the best restaurants, too. Food was one of Sam's desires.

"Girl, get up and let's go. I'm hungry, ain't you? Don't tell me you don't feel good—food will make you feel better. Come on, call Joan or your mother. I'm ready to go!" Sam was persistent.

God spoke very strongly to me one day while Sam, Joan, and I were driving down in Randall, Ohio, looking for an address. I heard God when he said, "*turn around and go back home.*" It was strange because for some reason, I headed back.

"Hey, how did I get on this side of the road? It's going east, and we were headed west on Route 70. Oh, I'll go up and find a median and head back, going west to Randall."

We laughed and I found a median some miles up the road. We had been reading and discussing the Word. Finally, we turned onto the road that would carry us to the address. All of a sudden, we were hit in the back of the car. I saw the hand of God grab my steering wheel, turning the wheel causing us to slide down a small embankment into an apple orchard. The car had been hit severely by

108

the rear. The motor was running as if to explode. Then I heard that voice say, *"Turn the motor off with your key and get out your door— the only way out. Move quickly!"*

I moved fast and yelled as I got out the car, "Get out fast!" We had help immediately rush to assist us.

"Get that old man, hurry get him out!" I said.

Before I could say another word, I heard Sam say up in front of me, "What old man?"

I don't know to this day how he got past me without legs. He wore a prosthesis and when I heard him say, "What old man?" I passed out for a few seconds. At this point I was placed on a stretcher and was carried to the ambulance. I saw Joan with the green apple in her mouth.

"Girl," Joan said, "don't leave me out here all alone! I don't like apples that much!" She fell to the ground so as to be able to get into the ambulance with me. How could I be the one hurt while watching she and Sam? In the emergency room we were examined and told we would be okay. Joan could have stayed, but she didn't want to.

Sam was the best friend I had ever had. He was more like a father and I hold many of our funny moments in my heart.

***

Only fate could bring Ricky back into my life. A least seventeen years had passed, but there he was walking in the downtown area where I'd parked, waiting for my girlfriend to return from paying her bills.

"That sure looks like Ricky walking this way," I thought. Joan, too, was about to enter on the passenger side. With her door opened, I looked Ricky right in his face.

"Richard, what are you doing around here?" I yelled.

He stopped and yelled, "Oh God, it's Sylvia!"

I jumped out of the car and we both hugged, greeting one another.

"Hey, I live on Hudson Street with my lady."

The last time I remember was we parted happily to have seen one another once again. Hudson Street was well-driven by me for I took that route almost daily going to the grocery store or the mall out on

Market Street. Only twice did I notice Ricky working in the yard, but that was only in passing.

A new person now came into my life and brought with him yet another tumultuous situation. An acquaintance of mine from another church sent her son Michael to my place. He needed a place to stay for two days and so I offered him a room at least until his wife, G.G., came from New York. A family two blocks away had agreed to board Michael and G.G. when she'd arrived. But by a series of circumstances, the family had gone on vacation and forgot to leave the keys for the couple. So I agreed on a 'temporary' basis only— unfortunately this turned into a three-month stay.

It was during those three months that Michael brought a friend over—which surprisingly turned out to be Ricky. A few weeks later while hanging out together, Michael told Ricky how he and his wife G.G. had planned to 'do me in,' and would Ricky help? Instead, Ricky came to my home and asked if he could watch television until Michael and G.G. returned home. While Ricky's watching television, Michael and G.G. arrived.

"Over my dead body, man!" Ricky said to Michael and G.G. They had a few words. This is the first time I'd told them to leave…and they soon did.

Thereafter Ricky with force, began to visit more often and my daughter-in-law, after meeting him, developed a crush. So much so, that she'd gotten him a job where she worked. Ricky and I would often talk about how cunning she was.

"Oh girl, she's young. She doesn't know what she's doing," Ricky assured me he could handle his end if I could handle mine.

But jealousy soon overpowered my daughter-in law. She'd soon upset my spiritual life and called me for three straight days trying to make me understand that my son Lee had been molested by a very close, and prominent man from the church, during his teen years.

"Girl, what are you saying to me? Lee is less than a man because he laid with—? When? When he was quite young? Is that what you're saying to me? Yes, I let him spend nights and saw nothing wrong with that," I told her on the phone. By now I became so upset, I jumped off my bed and gave the receiver to Ricky. Running, I could feel him running behind me.

"Syl, stop! Don't do this! Where are you going?" he pleaded.

I took off in my car driving to the truck stop. There I ate and drank coffee until early morning. When I returned, Ricky was waiting and he gave me a good talking to, which set my mind in order to where I could stand up and face the issue that would soon follow.

By a series of events I soon confronted the issue of the choir director who had molested my son Lee. This would not be easy as he was the brother of the Bishop. I went to the Bishop with my story and he assured me he'd take care of things on his end.

Three years had gone by and within those years Ricky assisted me with the church and remodeling its basement in Niles, Ohio—but my Bishop did not favor him because he knew Ricky was on drugs—a fact I just didn't recognize, or maybe didn't want to. He would not accept Ricky or our engagement and we soon would break up.

"Syl, go back to church and forgive all those who wronged you. I can't hang, I tried, but the church ain't my speed, like Bishop said, I ain't the one."

He took off in my car and headed for Detroit. He was to return in two days, but I finally had to end up reporting the car stolen, never seeing Ricky again.

MY SONS

Marvin, my first son was born on March 27th, a small baby that could fit in a small box at birth. He grew quick gaining the required five pounds before he could come home from the hospital. I remember the day he would lay eyes on his father who had brought Marvin at 1-1/2 years old, his first and only toy, a tricycle.

"Mom, who is that man, my daddy?" Somehow Marvin sensed it was his father, but I replied, "It's a friend."

Thirteen years later Marvin got a chance to go visit his father on his part-time job off High Street. He came home so delighted. "Mom, that man's not a friend, he's my father and we are going to go places like fishing on a boat. From that day on, Marvin was full of hope, only to be let down after his father got married. Somehow I landed on the same street Marvin's father lived and one morning I looked out my front bedroom window and saw Marvin's father's wife pacing up and down in front of the house I was renting. By now Marvin began to show depression and would not answer my questions I asked.

"Mom, leave me alone."

He got worse, but soon I moved off that street, but still in the neighborhood then back to Cleveland and back to my own apartment in Y-Town. Four to five years had passed. My two boys graduated and were living each on their own. Nelson in Cleveland, Marvin with my mother. Lee had attended tractor trailer school.

Alone in my apartment I recall one day the phone ringing. I picked up the phone and remember the voice on the other end.

"Come to the Southside Emergency Room. We have your son Marvin Matthews. He has a bad injury to his leg."

When I entered the hospital ER, it wasn't strange to see it crowded. I paid little attention to the people who had gathered, nor did I see anyone I knew. The guard lead me back inside to the nurse's station.

"May I help you?" The nurses were busy running back and forth.

"Yes, I'm Marvin's mother. Can I see him?

It seemed as if everyone stopped and looked towards me.

"Oh, Mrs. Matthews, have a seat."

"What for, I just want to see my son. Where is he?"

The nurse had come out to place me somewhere so she could make me understand. "I see you don' t know. Please sit down."

"No, what is going on?"

The nurse paused, then she began. "Marvin is in critical condition and will be going to surgery to replace his hip. The accident was bad.

"Well, how are the other people?"

"They're all dead. The grandmother and her three granddaughters. Marvin was pulled out of his car after they used the jaw's of life. He'll be okay after his hip is replaced.

My knees bucked. "Show me where my son is."

When Marvin's eye caught mine, he said, "Mom, how are the other people? Is it true they died? I didn't mean to hurt anyone. Look at me. Why didn't I die too?"

By now, tears flowed down his cheeks. Marvin was charged with vehicular homicide and went to jail after he was able to be transported. This is when I learned the law. After a child turns eighteen, as his mother, (he was now in his early 20s) I could do very little, so I found a lawyer to represent Marvin. During Marvin's trial he was given a reduced sentence. But as we were leaving court, a man approached the lawyer and threatened Marvin.

"Man, see my face. I promise you're a dead man. Don't pass me on the street." That same man the following Sunday dropped dead at home.

Drugs would soon destroy Marvin's mental capability. He started doing strange things like stabbing himself in the chest nearly piercing his heart. Police several times came to place him in a straitjacket taking him to a mental hospital where he was stabilized with medicine. This went on for years. One day while at Parkview Counseling, his counselor told Marvin if he didn't want to take those shots or meds, he didn't have to. From that time on, Marvin refused his medicine and would act out daily. By now I had taken Marvin out of a boarding house and placed him in my home Sam willed to me, hoping this would help. Because I was a foster parent I could not permit Marvin to live with me, plus before I became a foster parent, Marvin had harmed people who came around him. So I found another home. Taking him out to lunch at a favorite buffet, Marvin did odd things, like place his hands up the dress of any lady or reach down to

113

feel the leg. Several times I would usher Marvin out of a restaurant refusing to take him any place for fear of what he would do next.

For instance, in church Marvin sat beside the biggest, darkest man and sucker-punched him. He at one time sat beside a mouthy woman and slapped her. He was banned from that church but given another chance as long as I would be with him, but I couldn't make him stay near me. We called the police who carried him out and sometimes to jail, but they would not hold him. This was continuous. One day I had picked Lee up from the bus stop and carried him to the home Marvin was living in. After knocking, Marvin opened the door to let us in, but the neighbor across the street asked that I come over to speak to her.

"Mrs. Cohen, did you know the police are looking for Marvin? He beat a man half the night with a bat. The man is in intensive care."

As she spoke I looked and saw a shoe in the street. "What do you mean? Marvin's in the house. I'll go over and see what he did."

As I approached the porch, I saw a splatter of blood and a belt. Once in the house, I asked Marvin and he acted like he didn't know what I was talking about until I saw Bert's sweater (the man he had beaten), and other clothing. As I picked up the phone to call the police, Marvin approached me with a kitchen knife up his sleeve.

"Look out, Mom," Lee yelled, "Marvin is about to stab you!"

"Oh Mom, I ain't gonna hurt you."

He began to run about the living room. By now the police had arrived. Marvin was soon released because the boy he'd beat refused to press charges.

"Mrs. Cohen, Marvin was my friend and I can't. Bert's sister also tried to get Bert to press charges, but couldn't convince him either.

Marvin soon set that house on fire—it was one thing after another with that boy. I was forced to sign that home over to a friend who was a carpenter. The city would have charged me four thousand dollars just to level it, money which I did not have—and so my friend saved that home.

****

Nelson, born eleven months apart from Marvin was a preemie, too. He was seven months and weighed close to four pounds. The only father he knew was my first husband, who Nelson met after Brandon came out of doing eighteen months in Fort Leavenworth, Kansas. I would not let my husband chastise my boys if I could help it. There was a time Nelson received a scar on his shoulder by a hot skillet.

One day I had been out for a few moments. As I opened the door to enter the house, I could see my husband placing the boys in a tub of scalding water.

"What are you doing!?" I yelled running up the stairs into the bathroom. We fought. "Give me my boys. You can't do this to them! The water is too hot!" I even went to the police station asking for some help. They took my story down, but never did a thing. Even after I was severally beaten myself, did I get help from anyone. The police that night had come to the house and refused to do anything. So I remained and tried to save our marriage.

It was not until we moved to Y-Town that Nelson would bring Jerome to the apartment.

"Mom, this is my dad and he wants to ask you a question. Mom, just say yes."

Jerome explained how he and Nelson were getting along just fine. "Sylvia, I know it's sort of late, but will you marry me. I have a girl I plan to marry from the church, but I want you to have the first chance. This will make Nelson happy and me, too."

Jerome seemed so sincere, but I simply said, "No, I ain't ready to join or be that church lady."

Nelson came over and said, "Mom, what did you say?"

"Nelson, I'm not ready for marriage. Maybe later on. Right now, no."

Nelson turned away and didn't say anything about it ever again. So when Nelson got married, I knew very little about it. Just that the girl was pregnant and they got married through the church. Nelson soon carved a life out for himself. He went to college while he lived in Cleveland and just did his thing. His wife was pregnant every year for five years. Nelson was a good husband doing all he knew to care for his family. They were in church, kids and all, and each Saturday, his wife was given free time. I would keep the grandchildren each summer they were returned, after we came from a family reunion.

One day my son would go to work at University Hospital. When he came home this one evening, the house was empty. His wife had left him. When he finally met up with her, she was with an old boyfriend and had applied for a divorce. Nelson told me how her man ran him down the street with a machete. How the children would cry to be with their father. How her mother took her to the hospital where she had her tubes tied without his permission. The kids are pretty grown now and Nelson lives with his second wife there in Cleveland. He's doing just fine now.

***

My third son Lee was also a premature baby. Born September 27, 1962, three pounds, eight ounces, but he was a healthy baby which they released to me after he'd gained a pound and a half. It was the following year that I moved to Ossing, New York, leaving my sons with my mother until we found an apartment. Lee's father was rough with him, but Lee was spared the bruises until one day his father judo-chopped Lee in the face. I was awakened by the screaming of the other boys.

"Mom, come quickly!"

I found Lee with the whites of his eyes showing. His tongue hung from his mouth and stains of blood was dried under his nose. He was rigid and stiff.

"Oh God!" I said as I picked him up shaking him up and down. "Lee, wake up! Lee!" Then I reached for the phone. "Operator, please send the police. My son is dead! Send help!" The operator tried to calm me down. The police are outside your apartment. I rushed, leaving the boys with my neighbors across the hall. At the hospital, Lee was taken out of my arms as the attendants pulled the curtains and began to revive my son. Lee managed to make it through.

Later, in school, he won an 'Artist Contest' that made it into the newspaper. But sadly, I lost that artwork. He went on to tractor trailer truck school in Pennsylvania. This I didn't want him to do, but by now I had very little to say since he planned and got married to a girl who had trapped my son. I would not attend the wedding. That marriage didn't last long. But one day I received a call to sign for Lee's leg to be amputated. His truck had jackknifed and he was dragged out the cab of his truck. The car that had driven behind him, ran over the top of Lee as he was dragged down the road. At the hospital, I fainted when I saw my son Lee. It was horrible. Wires protruded from a swollen body that didn't even remotely resemble Lee. He should have been dead. Sixteen hours of surgery saved him. It was a sight no mother should ever see. I was only to go to Jacksonville, Florida to pick up his body, but he lived through it all. I stayed with him day and night until his father came for a few days. Lee requested that his father would come down, too. When Brandon entered the room, I left. Maybe Lee thought we could come together again. No way!

Lee soon returned to Y-Town and went into a nursing home to recuperate. While there he met an attending aide who would take him home to live with her. She was after his money. Later on, for some odd reason, she was killed, but I had removed Lee from her place to Sam's home. One day I felt the need to go and sit around Sam's home. Lee had been expecting a $80,000 check by Fed-Ex for the accident. I was there when he got the check—but so was a friend of his who took Lee to where he wanted to go. Within five months Lee spent that money foolishly. I asked Lee for $10,000 to buy a home for him, but he cussed me out and wound up giving me $2,000 and said to get the "hell out of my face!" Lee sold all his furniture and not long after that he needed a place to stay again. Sam and I would let him room with us one more time. Later on, Lee did get married to a girl he'd met in church. To my dismay, he returned back to driving that tractor trailer truck. Now married, his life was restored to normal with one son they called Emmanuel, which meant God with us. Another son, Joshua, born two years later, Lee would be on his way to a strong, prosperous life until he shared his most-kept secret to his wife, how he'd been sexually abused, at which time the walls came tumbling down for me. Even today, it still rips at my heart. Why didn't Lee seek professional help? Why haven't I done anything? Because Lee was of age when it was told to me, nor was this done to me. If I say, 'oh well,' I say I'm waiting for justice to take over. God is just.

Sylvia J. Cohen

AN OPEN LETTER TO MY SONS

I feel so bad to have to say this about my children. Seems they were cheated out of life by my mistakes. Should I had placed them in foster care they may have gotten adopted and lived differently. But what is normal? Surely there are rights and wrongs. Consequences and blessings. But we all must stand on our own two feet.

Marvin, my first son, didn't get a chance to have two parents to nurture him with love and proper guidance. I was his only hope. I watched Marvin beg just to be with his father for a few moments. I could not direct him to see it any other way. Marvin, your father took out his pleasure to rape me. This is how you were conceived. Your dad had no intention to be a dad/father, or any other thing for you. Sure, when he was single, he made you a promise, but after he married that hateful woman who never cared, you were out of the picture.

Marvin, you needed fatherhood. I wish it was different. But, son, be your own man. You, too, fathered a child. What have you done for him?

The accident where children died should have taken you too. How dare I say forget it. You'll never live that down. Punishment can be too great for you to bear, but you must look beyond the hills for help, it's there for you. I can't imagine how being a man and never been loved by your own woman. Yet, you son, are full of love. I saw how you reached out to the wrong girls. Oh God, it hurts to see you trying to show how if given a chance, you, too, could love.Remember sitting behind school with glue in a bag and then heard the voice of God say, *"Marvin, put that down."* Yet, those laced pills later on would overtake your body until now you have no mind because the demons have taken root. I gave up my home so you could feel you belong, but you set it on fire. Now you're completely out there on your own. But isn't that the recycle of life? We all must give an account for ourselves. Those shots did stabilize you. Why didn't you simply take them? Each time you refused, there were consequences. We couldn't live together because I had foster children and couldn't trust you that you wouldn't 'abuse' them. Since then you have done so many things and the last, you tried to stab me. That, Marvin, was the straw that broke the camel's back.

I pray God restore your life, back to normal.

*****

Nelson, you were always your own person. This was good. I was so happy when you married and gave me such beautiful grandchildren. Clearly, I tried to be there for you, but time tells all things. They are pretty much grown and out of the way or should I say, in the way? The proof is in the pudding. Five girls and one son doing good to see them up, yet hanging around. Hey, that's what should be going on. Sorry I never got to be closer to your wife, Paula. She was spoiled. But poor Kim. I have very little to say. I only met her briefly at the wedding. Son, stay with God. Your father did all he could to point us in the right direction.

One thing, Nelson. You had to experience your children pulling, holding onto you and not let go. I remember one picnic how Jessie wanted to be with you. Aren't you blessed to have loved and then be loved. It's like a wheel that goes around. You gave true love and it came back. What an example. Hey, hold enough for those grandchildren will one day come. (*Smile*)

****

Lee, you were the last child and I hate to say that your dad was so immature. Don't let him turn you bitter. Stay out of the way. I pain to think how as a teenager, I permitted you to hang around a person I had fully put my trust in, only to find how he ruined your manhood. I see him directing. I see times he became angry, too.

Today in my heart, I want to report this to the right people, for his punishment. Not only you, but just think how many more lives did he mess up. It's not my place—you should have turned him in years ago. Vengeance is not ours. God will repay. Hold onto God. See you in the rapture, your Mom, Sylvia.

In life, we will travel many roads and some will be smoother than others, but the lesson to be learned along the way is not how or where you started, but rather how you finish. On there few pages, I conclude this one chapter of my life, a conclusion that does not end my life, but simply take a break. During this intermission I will collect my thoughts, replenish my writer's supplies and prepare to begin again. After all, "The race is not to the swift...but to the one who endures to the end."

Throughout this book, you have read about some of my disappointments, downfalls and setbacks. I wrote not for you to have sadness over my past, but that you would celebrate with me for my victories. My life started with a second chance, nurtured and cared for by my parents until I reached the age of maturity. It is at this point that my life becomes uniquely different. Differences that came into play because of the choices I made. That's right, I can't blame anyone else from this point on.

About the Author

Born in Leechburg, Pennsylvania in 1942 in a home my father built with his bare hands—the only help he had was from my pregnant mother—I was soon to be born. Birth for me was difficult—the umbilical cord was wrapped around my neck, to which I was pronounced dead—but early the next morning, July 5th, I began to cry—and seemingly my life would be about the same—difficult.

Life as a child was spent mostly on the hills that sat overlooking the township of Leechburg. The country was the best, but Dad's jobs were most affordable for him to move us West into Youngstown, Ohio. We traveled back and forth, but by the time I was eight years old, Dad and Mom settled down on the south side—a steel mill city which meant work for my father.

At the age of eight, several things happened, but one thing in particular. We found out why I cried so much—I had Sickle Cell Anemia. Each year I suffered the agony of having one crisis after another, even through my pregnancies and marriages.

Despite all the illnesses and obstacles I've overcome, I was able to accomplish many things. Yet I never did the things like most teenagers, which is where I want to direct this story—my story—to all of you.

www.ingramcontent.com/pod-product-compliance
Lightning Source LLC
Chambersburg PA
CBHW051422280526
45785CB00003B/1127